Wisdom

From The Smiling Panda

Kushagra Singh

Copyright @ 2023 by Kushagra Singh

All rights reserved.

This book or any portion thereof may not be reproduced or used in any manner whatsoever without the express written permission of the respective writer of the respective content except for the use of brief quotations in a book review.

The writer of the respective work holds sole responsibility for the originality of the content and The Write Order is not responsible in any way whatsoever.

Printed in India

ISBN: 978-93-5776-787-3

First Printing, 2023

The Write Order

A division of Nasadiya Technologies Private Ltd.

Koramangala, Bangalore

Karnataka-560029

THE WRITE ORDER PUBLICATIONS.

www.thewriteorder.com

Edited by Pooja R

Typeset by Shreshta Veergandham

Book Cover designed by Keerthipriya

Publishing Consultant : Aishwarya Wanjari

Acknowledgments

Merely dwelling upon this subject makes me realize how no effort of ours is solo. Behind any achievement that we make in life, there is always some factor—people or situations—contributing to it.

Life has been incredibly gracious to give me a chance to write and share. I see it as an immense privilege and a blessing.

Any bit of gratitude that I express would fall short but I am still going to attempt.

I thank my father for being extremely supportive and encouraging. His support and gentle push to take writing seriously have made things easier.

Over the year, there have been a few incredibly kind and supportive friends who have read each and every article of mine and their continuous support has made this daring task of compiling some of my writings in a book possible.

Rohit, Mohit, Sheetal, Saurin, Rizwan, Mukund Hari Ji, Megha, Prateek, Anupriya, Roma, Tanishka, Karthika, Sravan Dada and Adee, Nandini, Vivek, Abhijeet, Aparna, Harshita, Prashant, Mansi, Anubha, Nishant, Krittika, Gaurav, Poorak, Sarvesh, Ish Gupta are some of the names that come to my mind who have always been so kind, encouraging, and supportive in my writing journey. Each of your small and big gestures or even acknowledgment of my posts and articles is deeply appreciated. Thank you.

As an erring human, I may have missed a few names. I will make it a point to thank you personally as well.

The team here at The Write Order surpassed my expectations. Right from the first conversation with Shubham, who was kind enough to accept the manuscript, to coordination with Aishwarya, the entire design and editorial team—Keerthipriya and Pooja—all of you have been prompt, kind, and efficient. I am very thankful that my first book is published by all of you. I am already looking forward to collaborating with you in the future again. Hey, there can be many parts to this Smiling Panda series.

It is God (Krishna) who bestows me with the ideas. Without the blessing of the divine, I would not have been able to type out even a word, what to speak of an entire book.

For a once-upon-a-time reticent and often scared and self-conscious boy like me, having a book out is nothing less than a miracle.

Faith and the right company can make anything possible.

Author's Note

First of all, thank you for purchasing this book and making an investment of your money and time to give this book and this author a chance to share some of my ideas. If you have just stumbled upon this book at a bookstore (or anywhere else) and are flipping through the pages, please do not deprive me of the chance to express gratitude to you.

I got a taste for writing when I started writing letters of appreciation for my friends. Encouraged by their kind response and my yearning to share and express, I started writing blogs.

(One of the reasons behind sharing this trivial piece of information with you is that if you do not like the contents of the book, please direct your hate toward all the people who nudged me into writing.)

I find it a big achievement to even be able to put this work out there.

I have tried to share my heart in the simplest and most genuine way I could. My wish and sincere hope is that the book offers you some useful reflections and ideas to enhance the quality of your life.

The various articles that you will read in the book are a compilation of my writings over the past three years. I wrote them all at different junctures of my life journey within these three years and you may find divergence of perception on some topics. That is because as an alive being continuously processing new experiences and ideas, I try and integrate those in my writings. The common theme uniting all the write-ups is a sincere desire to share learning from life, Vedic scriptures like Bhagavad Gita, Ramayana, Mahabharata, and even popular cultures.

The learning I try and share is based upon the idea that—for an observant person, anyone or anything can be a teacher.

Accompanying every chapter is a journal prompt. You will read me talking about the merits of journaling often throughout this book. I have also had the blessing to conduct guided 'Journaling Journeys' over the past few years. Spurred by the positive feedback from those prompt-based journaling journeys to help one express, I decided to put one prompt after or within each article.

I highly encourage you as well, to give those prompts a try. Doing so will make your investment of time, effort, and money on this book an even more fulfilling experience. Also, in the age of information bombing, only reflected knowledge/information can potentially be applied for the higher good.

I have endeavored to speak to you, dear reader, in a way I would like a book to speak to me.

As a human, you will find me biased toward certain things. I hope you will overlook those biases whilst remembering some of your own.

If you are reading a paperback version, it means the paper has come from trees and that means, for putting this book content out there in the world, there was an environmental cost. I am asking myself as I write this note—is the message I am trying to convey really that important?

Is it worth the environmental cost?

Is there more to the book than it just being a vanity project?

I, honestly, do not know the answer to any of the above questions.

I would also like to express that even if one chapter, one journal prompt, one page, or one sentence can resonate with each and every reader, I would feel supremely blessed.

—Kushagra Singh

From The Smiling Panda

Snoopy : America's Ambassador Of Kindness 1

Dealing With The Inevitable 'Redirections' Of Life 10

Everything Burns 17

You Should Definitely Talk To Someone 26

Why I Will Not Be Ashamed Of Expressing Myself 32

Divine Commitment 36

Unlearning And Learning : Part 1 42

Unlearning And Learning : Part 2 50

Seeking Shelter 55

A Mountain, A Cave, And A Coach 63

On The Need To Feel Seen 71

The Power Of Intent 77

The Merits Of Having A Personal God 81

Physical Fitness And Yogic Lifestyle 87

On Defining Purpose 97

Let Fear Find You And Do Not Be Afraid 102

Reflections On Slowing Down 113

Power Of Repetition 117

Source Lagwa Lo! 122

A Bit On Faith	129
On Connections	133
Take It Easy	137
The Art Of Feedback	141
Circle Of Goodness	148
Life Is Just Not Easy	152
Honest Confessions Of An Angry Man	160
Be Like Jack	173
Wish You A Happy Ending	177
Personal Power Leakage	182
Four Tips To Cultivate Inner Power And Freedom	187
I Won't Kill You But I Don't Have To Save You Either	194
We All Deserve A Jambvan	200
Death Talk : Part 1	205
Death Talk : Part 2	211
Gates Of Heaven And Hell	220
My Toothbrush Anxiety	225
Power Of A Gaze	230
Posing For Instagram	235
An Apologetic Wish	239

Snoopy :
America's Ambassador of Kindness

When I think of the most iconic "Peanuts" comic strip character, Snoopy, I think of joy, imagination, laughter, cuteness, and a penchant for life. These are excellent associations with an entity, wouldn't you say?

This may be strange or hard to believe, but I discovered Snoopy in adulthood. I saw this Peanuts feature film in an empty theatre as a twenty-four year old, back in 2015. Since then, I have been a huge Snoopy fan. I even got myself a stuffed toy and have kept it since as a symbol of all that Snoopy represents to me.

I remember when my childhood brother and friend,

Poorak, invited me to visit him in the United States. My agenda was to be able to visit two places apart from meeting him, of course—The Golden Gate Bridge in San Francisco and The Charles M. Schulz Museum (named after the creator of the Peanuts comic strip) in *Santa Monica*. Fortuitously, Santa Monica and the Charles M. Schulz Museum turned out to be about an hour and a half drive from San Francisco. So I could cover both places of interest in one visit.

I was on the last leg of a really tiring tour of the States and also encountered the powerful Pacific winds a couple of days ago while taking a short cruise tour around the Golden Gate Bridge and the Alcatraz Islands. As I once mentioned, the dialogue, *"Dilli se hoon"* doesn't always work. The context for the dialogue came from the belief that I was accustomed to Delhi winters, and San Francisco, no matter how cold it is, can not intimidate me, at least not in the Californian summer.

I could not have been more wrong. Life humbles you, and how!

The experiment of going on the cruise with a cotton tee and cotton jacket led to a severe case of cold and fever. Having just kept one day for the museum visit before flying to my friend on the other side of the enormous land mass, I could not also afford to rest.

And so, chanting Lord Krishna's name to derive strength and eating whatever bland vegetarian food options I could find in the hotel, I decided to proceed with my plan. Seeking the help of a gentleman at the hotel where I was staying, I fixed myself a ride to the museum.

Welcome To Charles M. Schulz Museum

The ride to the museum was comfortable enough. The impeccable quality of the highways in the states is not exaggerated at all. The driver was also kind enough to play Hindi songs for me during the trip. It is funny and cute to hear the song, **"Jab bhi koi ladki dekhu mera dil deewana bole, ole ole."** There's no better ode to a Delhi boy, anyway. Witty universe, very witty.

The first thing apparent on the visit was the absolutely calm vibe of the place. The museum was formerly the office of Mr. Schulz. I'd describe the place as an American 'village'. In the museum, they have:

- a gallery of some of the Peanuts comic strips
- a small theatre to screen some short animated videos of Snoopy and gang
- a section playing the biography of Mr. Schulz
- an activity centre for kids to come and create some artwork with assistance from the museum curators
- the office of Mr. Schulz preserved
- an ice skating rink, which was really cool to witness
- a warm puppy cafe (cute, right?) and,
- a store to buy Snoopy merchandize

Miss Jean

I lingered in the joy and amazement of my wonderful visit for a while before wondering how to arrange a trip back to the place I had to get to for work. I did not want to hail another phone taxi, as it was way too expensive. For some weird reason, Uber doesn't work for foreign nationals, and *Lyft*, another ride-hailing app, had my request for identity verification pending. Due to my poor health, all I wanted was a direct cab and didn't want to depend on any other forms of public transportation. Until then, I had relied on buses and flights to travel around America. I was even hesitant to seek the help of my kind friends and connections there, as I did not wish to burden them.

So, I went to the reception and was greeted there by this graceful elderly lady who must have been in her fifties, judging by her skin, greying hair, and a kind aura that only develops if you have seen more than a few decades of life. Miss Jean tried talking to a few cab companies and mentioned they were quoting way too much for my destination. I agreed, thanked her for her help, and decided to contemplate the mode of travel while sitting around a lovely mural across the hall from the reception.

What happened next will remain etched in my memory for as long as I live.

As I was fiddling with my phone, hoping against hope that Uber works, Miss Jean walked towards me and started enquiring if I could fix a ride or not. I told her about the Uber situation and thanked her again for her kindness. I also told her how much I loved the museum and how this was a dream come true for my inner child.

I was so stunned when she said, "I wish I could have given you a ride back, but here, take this little gift (a Snoopy stuffed toy) as a gift from our side and let Snoopy be your charm and guide to take you safely to your destination!" She even showed the way to the nearest ATM to try one last attempt at booking an Uber with cash while bidding adieu.

When I asked if there was anything I could do in terms of a positive review or something, she politely said, "You reach back home safe, and I am just grateful you could make this trip!"

I could only gape in disbelief and gratitude.

Pudina Hara And ₹1 Change

Years ago, in my teens, my mother asked me to get a strip of *Pudina Hara* from the nearby market. I didn't want to go as a live telecast of a Manchester United game was just a few minutes away. But I knew if I didn't go, my match-viewing experience would not be a pleasant one ; I ran at full speed to the nearby chemist general store.

While handing out the strip of *Pudina Hara*, the shopkeeper quoted eleven bucks. In my frenzy to quickly complete the task, I was only carrying one ten rupee note. I requested the half-balding, ugly-looking 'bhaiyya' (I'm incredibly spiritual in my judgments) to take the ten rupee note. I'll return in a short bit and give him the extra change. He replied in a stoic and somewhat sarcastic voice: "Sorry, get me change."

Abay ganje (insert some beautiful, poetic Hindi abusive words I can't write here), I wasn't buying a bar of chocolate or some packet of chips here. Pudina Hara can be classified as a medicine! Also, was the economy that bad during those days?

Since that day, I have never stepped inside that man's store. I have noticed though he has lost clients directly proportional to the hair loss on his head. (I'm highly spiritual in my observations as well.)

Random Acts of Kindness: Gift of God

The Pudina Hara guy didn't owe me a thing. But, one word of kindness and granting me the 'big favour' of letting me return the ₹1 credit later would have perhaps earned him a long-term client.

Miss Jean, for sure, didn't owe me anything. I was a foreign resident visiting her country for a brief period. The Charles Schulz Museum may not be everyone's top destination in the United States of America. Still, it doesn't have a dearth of fans or visitors within that nation. And yet, here she was, giving away a Snoopy toy worth $15-20 as a charm, being incredibly gracious to check in about how I plan on returning, and displaying a kind of hospitality that seems rare.

Maybe to the reader, that little act may not seem much. But from the perspective of a tourist in a foreign state—continents away from home, a thousand or so miles away from his friend within that state, in a physically sick condition—Miss Jean felt like *Shri Krishna's angel*.

Whenever I think back on the incident or am reminded of it, I can't tell you how abundantly my heart and soul send blessings to Miss Jean. I may never see her again, and she most certainly will not remember me, but one random act of kindness by her has immortalised her in my consciousness for as long as I'm alive.

As I write this, I also think about how such lovely humans end up being ambassadors and representatives to the nation they belong to.

The key idea here is that we never know how an act of ours can end up impacting another. I can now somewhat appreciate the tenets laid out by saintly souls about engaging in random acts of kindness daily or whenever possible. There is now even data-backed science to suggest that human experience and happiness are enhanced through giving, receiving, or even witnessing acts of kindness!

My entire American experience (and not just this particular incident) was a case study to rethink my ideas and opinions about things I have not personally experienced. What the mass media portrays about anything, in particular, can be so drastically different in experience—be it a faith, a nation, or a person.

To summarise, if receiving such grace and kindness feels like such an overwhelming blessing, I wonder how it would feel to someday be at the stage of doing such an act of kindness without any expectation of reward or remuneration.

Thank you for reading one of the longest pieces I have written on this medium. I hope it sparks something useful within you.

P.S. Special mention and gratitude to Vidhi Bhabhi and Mansi Ma'am for being my angels in fixing the then-sick man's ride from one place to another.

Journal Prompt: When have you been on the receiving end of an expected act of kindness? How can you pay it forward?

Dealing With The Inevitable 'Redirections' Of Life

I had to choose Air India for a trip to Benaras recently as that was my only option at my preferred travel time. I picked it up after much trepidation, as the Maharaja has been pillaged for decades thanks to neglect and mismanagement by the Indian government. While the esteemed TATA group has taken over, it is logical to expect that there will be some time before the airline can renew itself thoroughly.

Benaras is only about an hour's flight from New Delhi, so I didn't think twice before going ahead with Air India after almost seven years.

What could go wrong?

Just around landing time, our pilot informed us that

due to poor visibility, we would be hovering for a bit and landing may be delayed.

That's alright, I thought to myself. I will get through one more episode of "Only Murders In The Building" (Recommended by the Smiling Panda).

The following announcement was a little disconcerting, though.

The pilot said we are now redirecting to Netaji Subhash Chandra Bose Airport, Kolkata. One more episode was okay; I didn't expect to be watching the entire first season of the show.

Now, I have never before experienced 'this kind of redirection'. Even though I have experienced (as we all do) delays in arrivals and departures and so on. The common theme across all beings is me being a solo but fortunately prepared traveller. I always carry some movies and shows downloaded on my iPad, and of course, the Kindle is like carrying your library.

Another thing that got people jittery was a couple of security officers coming to the aircraft to establish the identification of everyone's belongings. In the utter confusion and chaos of the situation, they were actually about to confiscate a bag belonging to a crew member!

Internally, I wondered why on earth we were in this situation and what lesson Bhagavan Vishwanath (Shiva) had for me. Such pranks are more suited to my deity, Shri Krishna, dear Shiva. You, Bholenath, are the sweeter, simpler kind. Externally, I tried to portray calmness, rant a bit on my social media feed, and smile at the jokes and complaints of uncles and aunties around me who had little control over the urges of the tongue and the stomach. Their biggest concern did not seem to be when the take-off would happen or the status of visibility in Benaras, but rather, why are we not getting food?!?

However, call it writer's instincts or just me trying to create a piece of content from my ordinary life and events, I could recollect a story I heard about AC Bhaktivedanta Swami Prabhupada, and that also led to the ideation of this blog.

How Far Is The Temple From The Airport

Once Srila Prabhupada and his disciple traveled from one place to another in America. Swami ji, being a devotee and sincere practitioner/acharya of Krishna bhakti was softly chanting the *mahamantra* on his beads:

> *"Hare Krishna, Hare Krishna*
> *Krishna Krishna Hare Hare,*
> *Hare Ram Hare Ram*
> *Ram Ram Hare Hare."*

Suddenly the plane started wobbling, and people started shouting and crying. Even the luggage from the overhead cabins began falling. Swami ji, however, was of a grave disposition and continued with his chanting. After a few minutes, the wobbling stopped, and the pilot announced they were safe, and now people clapped and cheered. Once again, the disciple noted that Swami ji continued chanting unfazed. The disciple was in a quandary. How can Swami ji not even make a single comment? It did seem like a matter of life and death!

Later on, when they got off the aircraft, Prabhupada's only question was, "So, how far is our temple from the airport?"

Reaction Or Response

For a saint like Prabhupada, whose mission in life and faith in the divine are so clearly established, even matters of life and death cannot sway them.

However, for the more ordinary like me, and assuming you, dear reader, fall into the same category, even a simple redirection of flight can cause jitters.

What can we best do?

A situation like the one I faced with the Air India flight is out of anyone's control. I can bitch about Air India or the weather or blame my selection, which again was forced due to lack of choice anyway, but neither brings any solution or relief.

The best, when faced with life's inevitable redirection, is:

- to say a silent prayer
- ask for guidance and patience
- be prepared for such times in the lesser turbulent times
- be grateful even amidst the reversals

Let me elaborate a bit more on every point a bit more.

Saying a silent prayer is often a display of surrender. Hey, I cannot do much in the situation or predicament I am in. Dear God, help me. Seeking guidance and patience is also an addendum to a prayer.

When I say we should be prepared for such events in less turbulent times, it is like me carrying movies and shows downloaded on a device, having my Kindle and books (even for an hour-long flight), and also trusting my intuition to keep a couple of food items in my backpack before I left home. This is obviously applicable only for travel, but we use our imagination to prepare for any challenging situation that may or may not come to pass. Stay prepared. It is like when we get life insurance done assuming still that we will live a long life. A car insurance is also mandatory, and we hope to never make use of it. In easier times, it is always advisable to work more on our mindset and soak it in wisdom to make it stronger.

And lastly, the राम-बाण (Sureshot) solution to almost every issue in life is gratitude. While I sat there lamenting that a one-hour flight had turned into a five-six hour flight, I failed to notice something more important: this was just a redirection and not the end of the journey! While we only landed at a destination we did not want to go to and that too for a brief span, there could have been several things that could have gone wrong—like the flight not landing at all!

To conclude: life will always throw redirections and unexpected challenges our way. But one who is prepared will find it easier to navigate and deal with them than one who is shocked and overwhelmed. Breathe, surrender, pray, and be grateful.

Thank you so much for reading until the end of the

piece. I hope you enjoyed your investment of time. If you did, please share it with others you feel may enjoy such reads.

Journal Prompt: When did a redirection or setback in life turn out to be a blessing?

Everything Burns

"You're a shameless man, brother."

Vidura was never known to mince words. And also one who always aligned with the truth. When no one spoke at the shameful and dishonourable incident of the attempted disrobing of Draupadi, only Vidura had the guts and strength of character to challenge the assembly.

It is a testament to Vidura's character that when Bhagavan Shri Krishna was concluding his Leela (human incarnation) on the planet, he thought of Vidura and even left him a message. Poets and saints have also immortalised how Krishna chose to have a simple and humble meal at Vidura's house, rejecting Duryodhana's fancy offerings devoid of love.

Vidura was one of the most venerable and iconic

characters in Mahabharat. As a (step) brother and friend to the blind King Dhritarashtra, Vidura always gave the best and, often, unpalatable (as perceived by the blind king) advice to Dhritrashtra.

The Mahabharat War is described to be one of the most gruesome wars to have ever been fought among humans on earth. In more than one way, there was divine intervention involved as well. (A certain chariot driver who was there in the war is popularly known as God in human form in the land of Bharat.)

Before the war, Vidura had renounced the kingdom, for he couldn't bear to witness the injustice, blatant idiocy, and war-mongering by the Kauravas headed by Duryodhana. He went on a pilgrimage as the eighteen-day war was planned, fought, and concluded. Once he returned, Vidura was shocked to see Dhritrashtra finding comfort and joy now in the company of the very people he had wanted to eliminate at one time!

"How can you be so shameless? You did everything in your power to try and kill the five brothers. You allowed their wife to be mistreated amidst a full assembly. In the war, Bhima single-handedly killed all of your sons. Yet you continue to live amongst them. Now when he drops you food, you lap it up like a dog. Oh, I wonder how strong is this Maya (material energy) of the Supreme Lord Vishnu that even at the very end of one's life, one cannot let go of the attachment to material comforts."

Paraphrased From Srimad Bhagavatam, 1.13

A modern mind may wonder what is so wrong with an elderly man living with his surviving family at the end of his life. However, in the context of that era, Vidura was spot on in admonishing his elder brother.

Unlike our modern-day generation, which is confused about genders and the filters to apply to their digital photographs, the Mahabharata-era folks were supposed to have more refined standards.

The people in that era followed what was called वर्ण-आश्रम dharma. This dharma propounded one to follow a natural progression from student life to household life and then, at the right time, relinquish your daily duties, cut your attachments to family, and move away to engage in austerities and meditation. The essence of following this code was that human life is meant to achieve four goals, namely, Dharma (righteousness), Artha (wealth, material goals), Kama (fulfilment of material desires), and Moksha (liberation). Separating yourself from family was to cut distractions in the quest for moksha, or liberation.

Vidura, as an ever-well-wisher of Dhritrashtra, was pained to see that despite the terrible losses that occurred in Dhritrashtra's life, he was not ceding control over the palace. Though Dhritrashtra had a lot of affection for Vidura, earlier, more often than not, he used to ignore the sound advice of his brother. However, after years and years of counselling, Vidura could finally get through to his elder brother. Through the bitter medicine of Vidura's words, Dhritrashtra finally awakened to the reality of his mortal existence. He and Gandhari sneak out of the palace without informing Yuddhisthira (so that he doesn't stop him from leaving) and move towards the Himalayas to attain liberation (the texts of the Srimad Bhagavatam reveal that they ultimately did).

An Icon (Diva) In Decline

I started watching football after getting addicted to a video game. FIFA'04 will always remain special, for it not only made me fall in love with football but also helped me gain my best friend, Poorak.

I remember watching bits of Euro 2004 and falling in love with two teenage footballers, namely, Cristiano Ronaldo and Wayne Rooney. Both coincidentally played for the same club, Manchester United.

I started following United and thus began a tumultuous, passionate, and emotional love affair with one of the most iconic football clubs of all time. My love-hate relationship with Manchester United has lasted longer than any other romance in this lifetime! United, during those days in 2004, was in a mini-slump. Many of the old stalwarts were leaving or fading. Chelsea under the Russian Billionaire Roman Abramovich and the enigmatic Jose Mourinho had stormed the premier league. However, within two years, Sir Alex Ferguson created one of the most dominant footballing teams the English top tier had ever seen.

Oh, the joy and sheer exhilaration that United and, in particular, Mr. Cristiano Ronaldo brought along. I have shrieked and screamed in ecstasy, jumped up and down (often much to the shock and chagrin of my parents in the other room) as I watched United take the league by storm. I was heartbroken and devastated when Ronaldo decided to leave United for Real Madrid. My loyalty was to United, but I kept a close and envious watch as Ronaldo smashed records, won record-breaking Champions leagues, and became the most iconic football player of this era along with Lionel Messi.

When Cristiano Ronaldo unexpectedly returned in August 2021, it was a carnival! The fans were psyched to have arguably the best player they had ever seen in a United shirt back home. So what if he was 36? I can't tell you how many times I have jumped around doing the man's iconic SIUUU celebration.

Spoiler alert: this reunion or homecoming didn't have a happy ending.

Re-signing Ronaldo was supposed to catapult United as serious contender. However, that season turned out to be one of the worst ever in the premier league era. While Ronaldo scored the most goals for the club in the season, the team suffered. Many pointed fingers at Ronaldo's extraordinary stature and a lack of suitability to the fast-paced premier league as a clutch for the football team. As the season ended, reports emerged that Ronaldo wanted to leave the club. What seemed like a dream come true turned sour swiftly.

Ronaldo, who earned half a million pounds per week (read that again and do the arithmetic) at United, couldn't find another club to match his extraordinary wages. Media reports also suggested that most of the elite clubs in world football rejected overtures by

Ronaldo's agent, as they, along with any reasonable football fan, understood: The Icon is in decline. The new manager of Manchester United, who seems like the smartest appointment the club has made post the legendary Sir Alex, refused to indulge in the diva, oops, I mean icon. Once again, anyone with even a modicum of football intelligence could see that the team played much better without Ronaldo than with him. Only Ronaldo and his army of internet fans refused to believe it.

Just before the start of the FIFA World Cup 2022, Ronaldo did an interview with the controversial Piers Morgan. In that interview, Ronaldo hit out at his critics, calling out names and insults to ex-teammates who dared to criticize him. He also launched an attack on the club (in parts, rightly so) and the manager (uncalled for). As it stands, his contract and reunion with United ended sourly.

Time : The Ultimate Power

Bhagavan Shri Krishna, while revealing His universal form to Arjuna in the 11th Chapter of the Bhagavad Gita, says:

कालोऽस्मि लोकक्षयकृत्प्रवृद्धो (11.32)

"Time I am, the great destroyer of the worlds..."

Kassius Klay, whom we know as the legendary boxer Muhammad Ali, was known for knocking out his opponents with a single punch. He proclaimed he was the greatest. And so it seemed when he was young and at his peak.

But, as the Joker in Nolan's Dark Knight said, "Everything burns."

The same Muhammad Ali who could knock out opponents with a single punch faced a struggle to light up the Olympic torch at the 1996 Summer Olympics as he was diagnosed with Parkinson's syndrome.

We can be the greatest like Mr. Ali, Mr. Ronaldo, or just about any ordinary person, time humbles us all.

Some may argue, though, that the relentless pursuit of greatness mixed with a bit of cockiness makes these athletes reach dazzling heights. But then there are stars like Sachin Tendulkar and Roger Federer, who are venerated more than others not just due to their immaculate sporting achievements but also their humility and arguably timely exit from the top level.

It is a sobering thought that if such great personalities end up seeing a decline in their powers, what of us, ordinary mortals?

The idea is not to compare ourselves with stalwarts, poke fun at them or judge a legend's downfall. The intent has to be to learn that while gifts may be taken away and talents may wane, the thing that ultimately matters is your inner growth and that of your character.

May we be inspired to cultivate, harness, and ideate the facets that have longer durability than fame, possessions, and attachments.

P.S. The Smiling Panda recommends watching the Dark Knight Trilogy.

Journal Prompt: When have you experienced the humbling power of time in your life?

You Should Definitely Talk To Someone

I like running. It is an activity that helps me process a lot of emotions, engage in a focused, meditative act, and gain some cardiovascular fitness. I'm not a pro-runner, though, and primarily run for recreation.

Curiously, I have started enjoying running more since my formal yoga training. Running was introduced to me by a dear friend, Sudhanshu, back in 2010 or so. Since then, running has been a fallback option if I am not engaged in any other fitness activity.

When the COVID restrictions were lifted back in 2020 here in India, I was not at my best regarding physical fitness. Before my yoga teacher's training, I used to treat fitness as something I would indulge in only when it was an absolute necessity, judging by the number on the weighing scale. I didn't understand that fitness is a way of life and not an indulgence catered to a specific goal. Anyway, that's a topic for a separate piece or podcast.

I have always had an affinity for yoga, so sometimes I used to do a few Surya Namaskars, and once we were allowed to go out, I started going to a nearby garden to run.

However, I noticed that even though I was wearing proper running shoes and good-quality socks, the skin between the toes used to get chafed mid-way through the run. I couldn't quite understand why it was happening.

One day, when I met my dearest friend, Rohit, I casually shared my little grief. He suggested I try to moisturise my feet before putting on socks and shoes.

I obliged.

It has been almost two years since that incident, and I have never since had the same issue while running.

Sample Survey

Once during a workshop, the host asked a group of people how many presents here do a get-together with their close friends and talk about their lives, and so on. If not physically, then say, at least getting on a call and sharing and listening.

While this may sound clichéd, largely within that group, the number of women who affirmed doing so was more significant than the number of men. A prominent reason for this has to be the wrongly ingrained ideas of masculinity that can make either gender shy away from sharing. In earlier generations, talking about your problems and sharing them were not considered macho.

When the host further asked how they would feel if they were denied that chance to share?

The respondents said that if they couldn't share as much as they did, it would add to their collective stress and anxiety. Even the ritual of getting on a call or meeting a dear friend once a month helped them feel calmer and more peaceful.

While this cannot count as a 'scientific study' one cannot deny the efficacy of the truth in the survey.

The most desirable thing a human needs is someone to give them patience and present hearing. If there is one thing that can make a person endearing to another, it is the ability to listen.

The Inhibitors

There can be many things that may inhibit us from sharing our hearts:

- Fear of judgement
- What if the other is busy with their own life and doesn't have the time to talk?
- Fear of vulnerability
- Feeling of unworthiness
- Introverted disposition
- Thinking that our problem or anything that we have to share is insignificant
- Not having someone trustworthy or available to reveal our heart
- The trap of ego

My personal experience, owing to the blessing of Shri Krishna, has been that, more often than not, people are willing to help or hear you. More than we give them credit for.

This, of course, needs us to 'utilize' the blessing of having people around.

How do we do that?

By investing in the relationships first. By being present with them, serving them to the best of our ability, and being genuine in our intentions. As one of my spiritual mentors puts it, you need to invest consistently in relationships before you think of withdrawing.

I have also felt that sharing and talking with others also leads to humility.

When we're not exposing our thoughts and ideas to others, we risk becoming like a frog in the well. We might think our ideas and opinions are the be-all and end-all.

The adage goes, "If you're the smartest person in the room, you need to change the room."

I'd say that by not sharing and talking with the other people 'in the room,' we risk the trap of ego and the assumption that I'm the smartest in the room. Sometimes the ones who are least expressive end up knowing a lot more.

For instance, in the Mahabharata, Sahdev (one of the Pandava brothers) had the blessing of foresight. He was the most knowledgeable of the five brothers. However, he was of grave composition and hardly ever spoke much.

When we share our hearts with others, there is always a high probability of learning something new and getting a new perspective on our ingrained opinions. Of course, all of this added to the benefits of feeling calmer and happier.

A Personal Touch

I have always gained a lot of perspective and clarity, sharing my heart with some of my dear friends.

I learned that it is not always necessary for the other person to be in a zen-like state or have everything figured out for them to hear you and even share valuable inputs. All one needs is a compassionate heart.

Case in point: My friend Rohit, who'd advised me to moisturize my feet before running, isn't even a runner.

Lastly, it is also important to note that one can even converse with God. The learned ones opine that prayer is when you talk with God, while meditation is when you're listening to the divine.

Thank you so much for reading until the end. I hope your investment of time in reading the piece sparks a positive idea and enables you to share more.

Using writing as a tool to express.

Journal Prompt: Recall an incident where sharing something with a loved one had a significantly positive impact on your life.

Why I Will Not Be Ashamed Of Expressing Myself

I didn't speak much as a kid because I did not have the required confidence. The fear of judgement, bullying, and being made fun of inhibited me from expressing myself. It is also curious that hardly any teacher (or adult around) encouraged me. However, I won't blame them because no one teaches us how to deal with human beings; educating humans on fostering good relationships is not something deemed necessary in the rat race of life.

I have loved expressing myself since my teens. Then the opportunities did not come as much as I would have liked. By the grace of Krishna (God), I could find many opportunities to express myself in college and, subsequently, in theatre.

When I reflect on the previous decade of my life (the 20s), I realize I should have been more careful with words. Just because you have a blessing of an actively working vocal chord(s), and you know a language, should not mean you keep talking– especially speaking harshly or using your voice to cause pain or hurt to another living being. I am guilty of doing so on innumerable occasions.

However, barring the angry outbursts and caustic expressions, I have never been told that my verbal (or written) expressions created a problem for anyone.

I have a habit that I adore. I continuously try to update myself with the knowledge to improve. I'm a big fan of self-help. Thanks to this habit, I realized lately that I could be a better listener. I reflected upon many conversations with my friends and those around me and realized there is little active listening. Exchanges where one is actually interested in what the other person has to say are rare. I liken it to the time some of us used to play gully cricket. Everyone was desperate to either be the bowler or the batsman! No one wanted to field. Or, in a few cases, some only wanted to do the batting (talking)!

Over the past few months, I have been willing to apply my mind to listening when someone is talking. I am not always successful. My previously created and set habits of wanting to interrupt the other person with something I wish to say do crop up. But, because I've become aware and started improving myself, I see good changes, which makes me happy.

There is an interesting offshoot to this little practice of mine that I noticed, though. That's what prompted me to write this blog.

We may be aware of this voice inside us, which acts as a critic and keeps judging us no matter what we do. It may be the voice of an adult we had to endure as children, which became a set pattern in our subconscious. My inner critic has been a constant for a long time. A few years of therapy under able teachers and, of course, self-analysis, work, and good company have helped me identify it. Identification is one thing, though, and shutting it down is an entirely different thing altogether. It takes time. It IS taking time for me, at least.

So, as soon as I started trying to be a better listener, I felt guilty about expressing myself! So much so that I began to feel sorry about being expressive in conversations or talking (what I deem to be) too much.

Strange are the workings of the human mind!

It is noteworthy that no one else told me or pointed out that I'm speaking too much or that I should give my vocal cords a rest. Well, maybe they wanted to but were just kind not to do so!

I ask myself, 'Why should I or anyone else not express themselves when they can?'

Unless one speaks words full of malice, hate, putting others down, judging, abusing, gossiping, pushing a political agenda, or unnecessarily boasting about themselves, why should one not speak if they feel like doing so?

I have observed how good it feels for others when I have heard them out and allowed them to share earnestly. Becoming a better listener should not mean feeling guilty about your expressions.

So, dear reader, if you have something to share, to express, or to talk about, do it. Just know when to shut up if you feel that the person you share it with is not interested.

But, even then, you can journal, record audio, talk to your pet, a plant, a tree, or, best of all, God, if you have that faith and connection. Heck, talking your heart out to God can accentuate your connection to the divine, unlike any other method.

Most importantly, do not feel bad for what makes you come alive. I always emphasise that as long as what you do doesn't cause hurt or pain, you should do it. I took my example and realization around verbal expression, but for you, it could be something different.

Through this write-up, I have tried to remind myself of the essential wisdom of not being ashamed of your authentic self.

I hope you resonate and find meaning.

Journal Prompt: Where and how can you start expressing yourself without inhibition?

Divine Commitment

Srimad Bhagavatam is considered the crown jewel by scholars of Vedic scriptures. While one finds it to be replete with stories from *itihas*, astronomy, philosophy, creation, etc., it effectively outlines the biography of **Bhagavan Shri Krishna**. Please note that Srimad Bhagavatam is a *Purana* (set of ancient Vedic texts), which is different from the **Bhagavad Gita**.

अहो बकी यं स्तनकालकूटं
जिघांसयापाययदप्यसाध्वी ।
लेभे गतिं धात्र्युचितां ततोऽन्यं
कं वा दयालुं शरणं व्रजेम ॥

SB 3.2.23

"Alas, how shall I take shelter in one more merciful than He who granted the position of mother to a she-demon [Pūtanā], although she was deceitful and prepared deadly poison to be sucked from her breast?"

This verse is one of the most cherished by the scholars of the Bhagavatam. The learned ones explain that this verse highlights the compassion that God, Krishna, bestows upon even those who happen to be inimical to Him.

Now, this particular idea changes everything that we may have learned about God or religion from our exposure to the subject of God. When even taking God's name in vain can be considered blasphemous by some, how can someone who possibly had the motive to kill God not only get liberated but celebrated and immortalised?

The above verse challenges the ingrained idea of God being a hard taskmaster, existing only to dole out rewards or punishment and subjugate the dependent souls.

Here, the idea of God is filled with compassion, grace, and love for every living entity, regardless of their motives, actions, or intentions.

The Story Of Putana

In Chapter 6 of the book (canto) 10 of the Bhagavatam, we read the story of Demoness Putana coming to *Gokul* to try and poison baby Krishna.

The narrator *Shri Suka* uses two adjectives for her: and बालघातिनी for Putana, i.e., Ferocious and a literal killer of babies.

Krishna was only six days old since He had to face cold-blooded assassins like Putana who were out there to eliminate Him. And while other assassins who came later were usually direct in their approach, Putana was the most deceptive one.

Putana, taking on a beautiful external form to dupe the residents of Gokul (where Krishna resided), entered the *Nanda Bhavan* and tried to poison baby Krishna by feeding Him her milk.

That was her modus operandi: Enter the homes of newborn babies, smear her breasts with poison, and unbeknownst to the other family members, kill their babies.

The story has incredibly profound spiritual meaning and has had tons of masters write their commentaries on just one incident in baby Krishna's life. All of it is beyond the scope and capability of this author to elaborate on. I will humbly try to put forth my personal takeaway.

When the demoness tries her tried and notoriously tested technique to kill this particular baby, He not only drinks the milk but also suckers up her life.

सा मुञ्च मुञ्चालमिति प्रभाषिणी

(SB 10.6.11)

"Please leave me, leave me," cried out Putana.

Alas, she didn't know that the future butter thief, the speaker of the Gita, the enchanting flute player, never quits.

Ever.

Not even on the ones who wish to kill Him.

Not even the ones like us who have long forgotten our eternal relationship with Him.

The verse I quoted at the beginning of the blog is uttered by **Uddhav**, one of Krishna's most trusted friends and ministers in Dwarka. When Krishna leaves the earthly realm, He instructs Uddhav to stay behind. Uddhav, upon meeting **Vidura** (from the Mahabharata), breaks down, remembering the magnanimity of his beloved friend and worshipable lord.

Heartfelt relationship forged with animals and humans give a glimpse into the divine nature of love from which we emerge. I use the term emerge here because Vedic scriptures describe God as a manifestation of love.

But unfortunately, while true love is everlasting, bodies are mortal. Assuming that one has had the good fortune of forging an unconditionally loving relationship, the laws of nature separate either of the two. We observe that more and more relationships are becoming conditional and transaction-based. I am no one to judge, for I honestly admit to being attracted more towards those who fulfil certain mental, emotional, and physical needs! It is easy to antagonise even the closest relationships if they fail to live up to our expectations.

But here, the Vedic scriptures talk about a divine that never leaves you, no matter which form of life, planet, or condition one enters. Just like Krishna did not let go of Putana despite her pleas, our divine lover never quits on us, even if we abuse and desecrate the bond through our egoistic acts.

One cannot even think of committing the sins Krishna is willing to forgive. Just like a mother tolerates the baby's kicks in her womb, Krishna (or God) tolerates all of our mistakes, lifetime after lifetime.

While Krishna proclaims that the divine descends to establish dharmic principles and annihilate the miscreants in the Bhagavad Gita (BG 4.7), the spiritual masters explain the hidden reason. The esoteric cause of the descent of the divine is to give a glimpse of the eternal love that awaits the soul if it decides to embrace its divine essence.

The only takeaway I can offer you for your investment of time, dear reader, is to reflect on your personal relationship with the divine. Many, like me, find that source to be Krishna. For you, it may be the holy spirit, Allah, Rama, Jesus, Shiva, Buddha, or your soul itself. The definition is not as important as seeking to grow this relationship as carefully as we want our material wealth to grow. An intelligent person is fully immersed in the present but also plans for the future.

Our deeds, impressions, and relationship with the divine are the only things we carry forward when the body perishes.

The choice is ours.

Always.

P.S. I do warn you to tread carefully, though. Once the lure of the mischievous Murari (another name for Krishna) ensnares a soul, there is no letting go. Like a lover possessed, He won't stop until He wins your love. He just doesn't steal butter; He steals hearts as well.

Journal Prompt: Write about a time in your life when something moved you to such an extent that you felt some force much greater than yourself.

Unlearning And Learning : Part 1

The unpredictability of life is no longer a shock or surprise. If you're in the same boat, say aye!

Part of adulting is navigating through the surprises that life throws at you. I mean, we eventually do acclimatize.

Or do we?

If we observe within our circle of interaction and experience, we find some are more resilient to life's challenges, some crumble swiftly, some remain nonchalant, and some are blessed by dint of their previous and present karma that helps them stay afloat.

But, yes, the package of challenges knocks on each door.

The Bliss Of Ignorance

Have you ever found yourself thinking, 'Why didn't anyone teach me about life's challenges and unpredictability?'

I certainly have.

Formal education sorely lacks emphasis on making you a mentally robust human.

The majority of the parents, unfortunately, themselves, weren't raised to look after their spiritual and mental health. Our nation is still slowly crawling out of the 'occupational hazard' of Turks and Brits. For our previous generations, the emphasis was to find a decent-paying job and settle down. In effect, those are the values that they have passed down to us.

We tend to live so blissfully unaware of life's variables that it is astonishing!

Here's an example:

Death.

"What is the most surprising thing in the world?" asked the Yaksha.

"The fact that we see people die all around us and yet think of ourselves as immortal," replied Yuddhisthira.

(On the same note, Srimad Bhagavatam says a parent should start contemplating the mortal nature of life upon the birth of a child, and the child should contemplate its mortality when it witnesses the death of a parent.)

Death, like birth, is a constant in the world. While I humbly feel that nothing can prepare one for the eventual demise of a person they dearly love, it is disappointing that even opening up a conversation about death is avoided. Perhaps some superstition says that talking about death will signal its arrival sooner. Just like the funny (and also sad) idea that keeping the Mahabharata at home will lead to fights!

Another topic is dealing with failures—say at work, in relationships, in studies, or in just about any endeavour in life.

No one, *absolutely no one*, gets it right all the time. Be it any athlete, business tycoon, movie actor, politician, etc. A lifetime spanning many decades will always find errors, crashes, and ups and downs.

And, yet. And yet.

I'll hold my hand up and say that even as I write this, I know how difficult it gets for me to handle even something as innocuous as the failure of my favourite sports team (more on that in a blog in the future). And hey, I may rant about it on social media, but there are some 'wise ones' that end up destroying their television sets, burning effigies of their sports icons, or even issuing threats of violence on social media if their favourite team loses. And through this silly comparison, I find an excuse to continue ranting about my sports team. (Although their fortunes have witnessed an upturn recently. Praise the lord!)

But, in all seriousness, there is so much void that modern education and, often, our upbringing create.

So, where does that leave us?

Should we continue to suffer just because we weren't given a memo, or should we strive?

Rather than choosing to blame The Queen, Shri Nehru, our parents or anything else, let me share some important reminders that may help us in 'raise ourselves' once again

Timeless Reminders For Life

The itch to share is acutely potent among human beings. We are fiercely social. No person, unless they have had unfortunately harrowing experiences with beings of their species and have decided to make a generalisation based upon the experience, can be okay without sharing and having company.

I have often thought I would certainly pass on my learnings and experiences if and when I have a child. Considering that the idea itself is variable and subject to many conditions, I felt like sharing it with my kind audience, who end up lapping some of my ideas and encouraging me: something that I cannot guarantee that my future child will.

So here is a list of some of the most important points that I feel will help me navigate life's challenges as I continue to stay alive and live this incredible gift of life.

- People around you and your loved ones will die. Grim, yes. They will leave a void that no one else can fill. Yet they will. Prepare your mind and consciousness. If one truly can grasp this idea of death, it is my absolute belief that we will start living better and also act more kindly towards people in our lives. My tip: find an authentic teacher of the Bhagavad Gita.

- Death is one way for someone to go away. What if life takes someone away? People can walk out of your life when you least expect or want them to. It can be excruciatingly painful if you are attached. And as a human being, there is a 99.99% chance that you will get attached. Give your best, cry when they leave, but know the only constant in life is your soul, your connection to the infinity we call God.

- Parents bring us into the world. They pass on the best and the worst that they got from the generations before. Unless they have been outrightly abusive or toxic, never ever forget to offer your gratitude and respect. More so as both you and their age. And while we are at it, remind yourself of lesson number one again. Loving, toxic, healthy, ill, detached, or attached—whatever type of parents we have, they will depart one day before you if the law of natural progression applies.

- Invest in your health. Start small, start with your body. In time one habit of regular workouts will save you from a lot of anxieties in the future. Remember, movement keeps us moving in life.

- As you begin moving your body on a consistent basis, you can get the impetus to learn more about your mind. While moving the body is the first step in the right direction, there are various other significant steps to a robust mind:

  1. Company of genuinely kind and loving people. You find them by being one.

  2. Keeping up with commitments to yourself inspires self-confidence unlike anything else.

3. Investing in learning the yogic practices of asana and pranayama can be highly effective in aiding a healthy mind.

4. The next step of hatha yoga has to be meditation. Once you start practising pranayama, meditation becomes much easier. Essentially, we need to carve out some time to just be with ourselves.

- Learn to forgive yourself even if you cannot or do not want to forgive another being for something that they did. Self-forgiveness is extremely important. Not only does it save you from debilitating guilt but also makes you more aware of your actions. If we stop judging towards our own actions and rather view them with an open mind, we allow the universe to help us learn our lessons harmoniously. It is a constant, vigilant job. You've got to keep up. Because you will continue to make mistakes. However, with consistent self-work, you can ensure you make new mistakes rather than repeating old ones. Also, if we succeed at the above, we have a high probability of forgiving others as well.

- It's a no-brainer, but it's incredible how often we miss this and take it for granted: Invest in humans–especially those who invest in you. Running after those people or things that are elusive brings nothing more than misery and pain. While we choose to cultivate and invest in relationships that have been brought into our life organically by God, we feel a sense of safety, warmth, and joy. An idea that I realize I have understood a little later than I would have ideally liked is that fulfilling relationships are more valuable than any other human possession.

- Drop entitlement. The universe is not meant to please or cater to your needs.

- Read. God, just keep reading. If you are fortunate, you will find a treasure amidst books that will enrich your life in ways you would have never imagined. My tip: Look for the genuinely happy and holistically successful people around you or at least those who project that in their public lives. Ask, try, and learn what they read. Start from there.

- Holistic success means growth on all fronts: health, wealth, relationships, and spirit.

- Never hesitate to share uplifting, kind, and generous ideas. Resist sharing that which brings down your personal energy and projects hate in any way.

- Look your best. Only a rare few should anyway have access to your heart and hence, present your best to the world. Your outer personality matters a lot, unless you are a monk or a yogi living away from human civilization. Heck, even monks need to look clean and presentable!

Unlearning And Learning : Part 2

- Give people second chances. If they need any more, then stop.

- Love yourself enough to say no to the things that make you feel uncomfortable. You are not an actor in a Mountain Dew commercial. If your body resists something, don't indulge in it.

- Smell nice, groom, and bathe. Please.

- The content you consume can consume not just your time but also your consciousness. Choose wisely. If you want to be peaceful, joyous, and motivated, choose accordingly.

- There is no thrill in putting another person down, including you. If you feel another person behaves inimically towards what you think you deserve, be vocal about it. More self-love.

- People can tell your genuineness or lack of it. If they genuinely wish people well, you will have it reciprocated.

- Envy makes you a loser. You do not know anyone's story or what they did in this life or previous lives to deserve abundance in any form. Don't burn in jealousy. Celebrate others' success, or if that doesn't come naturally, ignore it and engage in mental gymnastics of gratitude and prayers.

- On the same note, others having more never translates into a lack for me. The universe is capable of fulfilling each one's desires.

- If you constantly endeavour to grow, happiness does not remain a utopian idea. Just like a stuck body of water becomes stale, humans need to keep flowing and moving from one state to another. The more you learn, the more you feel good about yourself.

- "If you can't handle me at my worst..." No soul should handle you at your worst. You're neither a child nor an obligation to any human being. Your behaviour is solely your responsibility, as is your state of mind. Excuses be damned!

- You can be a scientist in your day-to-day life. Re-examine personal beliefs, ideas, and opinions.

- There is so much wisdom in ancient practices. Not all are relevant in our time, but having a scientific temper will ensure we do not reject something for the sake of modernity. Try, practise, experience, and conclude.

- Oscar Wilde once said, "When I was young, I used to think that money is the most important thing in life. Now that I'm older, I know that it is." Spend appropriately, and be charitable, but seek out and learn how to grow your savings. Schools and universities will not teach financial wisdom. It is our prerogative to learn about wealth and its management.

- I have yet to come across anyone indisciplined who is truly wealthy. If I cannot grasp the concept that discipline equals freedom, I have little scope to succeed in life.

- On the same note, I have yet to come across a truly successful person who doesn't rise with the morning Sun and who is frivolous with their nighttime routine. While it is understandable that not all people are identical, the window of opportunity to grow that "sattva-filled" morning hours can provide is unmatched. Whether you seek God or material energy, the early morning hours can transform your life.

- Be curious about others, but please be sensitive. No one owes you any right to share every detail about their lives. Do not make others feel uncomfortable on purpose. Be wise and aware of not overstepping your boundaries, even if you deeply care–this is especially important in intimate relationships.

- Human touch is a beautiful thing; it is a gift from the divine. An aware human should always be mindful of the kind of touch one gives. Respect your body temple to not allow just about any sort of touch in your space. I elaborate on it in a podcast episode (Magical Power Of The Right Kind Of Touch on Wisdom From The Smiling Panda Podcast), which has been getting good feedback.

- A lovely lesson I learned from Spiderman (Aunt May): If you help someone, you help everyone. That someone can be yourself.

- Learn to be okay with being alone for the things you enjoy doing: eating out, traveling, movie time, etc. While undoubtedly the activities mentioned above are ALWAYS much more fun in the right kind of company; however that makes you dependent. Dependency is harrowing slavery. The only person to be dependent upon is Bhagavan Shri Krishna. (Insert the name of whatever you consider to be the highest or purest in your life.)

- Laughter and jokes are a gift. Sharing them with friends is also a blessing. However, jokes at inappropriate times can cause immense pain and lead to fractured relationships. Especially constant banter. I have noticed there are only a precious few people who can make jokes all the time and still be funny, and rarely does anyone take offence.

- A truly profound learning experience for me recently was an idea shared by someone. They said to stop bothering about what any politician or political party is up to. Their careers and life paths are sorted; please focus on yours. Mind-blowing. Unless we get paid for our political ideas and opinions, it doesn't make much sense to keep dabbling our brains and energies in low-vibration-inducing political chatter. Also, I have never met one happy soul who keeps their mind hooked on such stuff.

- Lastly, let us hydrate more and smile a lot more.

The above is a list that I feel will keep growing if I keep living (and learning). There was a time I used to flinch at all the mistakes and errors committed in the past. I now feel differently. If I cannot look back on the past and cringe, then that means I have been stagnant. Maybe I can even look back at the version I am now and have a few cringe-inducing thoughts. I already cringe thinking about the Kushagra from the start of this year, and I'm sincerely grateful to Shri Krishna for the constant updating of my software.

May your software keep getting the necessary updates.

Journal Prompt: Curate your own list of what you need to unlearn and learn.

Seeking Shelter

Any human being of any gender, pronoun, identification, nationality or religion should agree on probably one thing: Life is full of challenges.

Or should I say, a conscious being would undoubtedly agree?

I often wonder if every juncture, new avenue, and turn of life brings forth the seed of disappointment and challenge.

In the Bhagavad Gita, 8.15, Shri Krishna uses two terms to define existence:

दुःखालयमशाश्वतम्

(Temporary and full of misery)

Bleak, haha.

Before you read further, let me clarify that the purpose of this piece is not to make you feel depressed or sad. Maybe you are in a good phase of your life, and I pray to the divine that it may continue for as long as possible. If you are going through a hard time right now, I pray and hope you find the strength to come out of it super soon. By the end of the piece, I intend to motivate you to find your safe space amidst life's challenges.

The challenge is to face our reality honestly. To see where there are wounds, so we can heal them. To not live in denial and avoid pain.

"The most fundamental harm we can do to ourselves is to remain ignorant by not having the courage and respect to look at ourselves honestly and gently."

PREMA CHÖDRÖN

My observations about life and its inbuilt challenges come from observing my personal life trajectory and what my friends and family share about their journey.

Here are a few examples:

Two fantastic human beings who found each other have not managed to be in the same country since their union.

Another intelligent and pretty friend cannot find love, even as she slays every other aspect of her life.

A daughter struggles to balance work and duty (and

relatives) towards her father, who is battling cancer.

This person has all the money and status one may aspire to but no filial affection.

One famous cricketer can shake his body well in advertisements and Instagram reels; he is ultra-caring for the environment and has excellent skin but he can't seem to put bat on ball.

The list can go on.

A caveat is that I have no complaints about life. Life has been extremely kind and giving. By the grace of Shri Krishna, my teachers and those around me, I have trained my mind to appreciate more than moan and groan. This attitude of gratitude in itself is a potent remedy to immunise oneself against difficult life situations and gather strength.

Quest For Meaning

What exactly is the meaning of life on a personal level?

I pondered a lot over the above question, as I have had the luxury of solitude lately.

Do we really have a purpose and meaning, or are we just making things up and attaching meaning to them as we go along?

As I was mulling over these questions, I felt let down by myself and, on some counts, like a failure. Not as a person, fortunately. But failure in various life situations where I think I could have or should have been braver, wiser, and so forth.

Hindsight is both a gift and a curse, depending on which juncture of life we use it.

Daniel Kahnemann defines it best:

Hindsight, the ability to explain the past, gives us the illusion that the world is understandable. It gives us the illusion that the world makes sense, even when it doesn't make sense.

Life isn't consistent for anyone, right?

Perhaps it is not designed to be so.

Everything changes: seasons, moods, people, and trajectories. Amidst the consistency of change, the heart longs for shelter, a grounding base, a secure and safe dwelling, if you must.

Personally if it weren't for Shri Krishna and His teachings, I would not have any sense of meaning and purpose in life.

And just because I have an established base and shelter, I could find hope and inspiration to endure my challenges. One particular verse from the Bhagavad Gita became the shepherd that guided me towards the light.

Mind The Mind

उद्धरेदात्मनात्मानं नात्मानमवसादयेत् ।
आत्मैव ह्यात्मनो बन्धुरात्मैव रिपुरात्मन: ॥

BHAGAVAD GITA 6.5

"One must deliver himself with the help of his mind and not degrade himself. The mind is the friend of the conditioned soul and his enemy as well."

I chuckled as I read the above-quoted verse. It came at a serendipitous moment for me because I found myself plunging into the quagmire of negativity when I read it.

The appeal of Krishna's words and the message of uplifting yourself with the mind's help is crucial.

Constant vigilance is something one has to cultivate; otherwise, I find it is effortlessly easy to slip into a negative loop.

The negative loop begins with one mistake, one adversity, one issue, and if you're not aware enough to tackle the disease of negativity at that point, boom! Before you know it, you're engulfed by it.

"Life is a mess."

"Nothing is working out for me."

Here's the worst:

"Others have it so easy. I'm the only one struggling."

Training the mind to focus on what is working for you

right now through the practise of breath awareness, meditation, mantra chanting and expressing gratitude is beneficial.

Of course, each one has its own methodology. What works for me may not work for another.

(One thing with which I feel we can never go wrong is the physical movement of the body to shake off both the mental and physical static energy.)

Even more importantly, the essence is to find a 'shelter' or 'home' where the mind can rest after all the energy spent trying to survive another day.

For some, their shelter can be a deity, the divine, someone from the family or a friend, a pet, music, or a hobby. Whatever it may be, it is vital that one find it and cultivate a daily practise of seeking that shelter daily. To allow the mind to rest, replenish, recharge, and focus again on living yet another day, irrespective of whether the day brings joy or sorrow or a mixture of both.

What is your shelter?

Where do you feel that your mind finds peace and home?

Thank you so much for reading until the end of the piece.

I leave you with a quote from one of my favourite authors, Mr Matt Haig.

"To feel hope, you don't need to be in a great situation.

You just need to understand that things will change. Hope is available to all. You don't need to deny the reality of the present to have hope, you just need to know the future is uncertain, and that life contains light as well as dark."

A Mountain, A Cave, And A Coach

Linda Goodman, the author of some famous books on sun signs describes Sagittarians (my sun sign) as adventurous and outgoing people. While I mostly agree with some of the other things she describes Sagittarians, I found the 'adventurous' part off the mark for me. The most adventurous thing I seem to indulge in is watching **Manchester United Football Club**. I also remember having experimented with **Haldiram's** atrocious 'Ice Cream Soda' during my college days. That pretty much sums up my share of adventure.

During my yoga teacher training, our curriculum included a couple of hikes. I looked forward to the hikes to test my fitness level more than anything else. In the third week of training, we hiked to the top of **Kohos Mountain** surrounding the beautiful Govardhan eco-village, our yoga school.

I do not know whether it was the high from three weeks of living in a pure *Sattva environment*, the great company, being led by a fantastic teacher, being on a mountain that has existed way before any of us and shall continue to do so long after we are gone, or simply my sun-sign analysis being right, but I thoroughly enjoyed my experience.

Do The Dew

Our head yoga teacher (Anmol sir) is an amazingly inspiring personality. I would define him as wild and free. He loves nature, animals, mountains, fitness, and authenticity. From day one, I was drawn to his teaching methodology and connected amazingly well. But as all inspiring personalities have eccentricities, Anmol sir too has his. At the top of the mountain, there was this cave-like opening filled with what seemed like sludge.

Sir called it water.

After the hike, sir wanted us all to enter that slu... water, which he said would help in the hike down as that slu...water will help relax the muscles and so forth.

My South Delhi instincts were channelled to the hilt.

"Bhaaayaa hum aise jagah nahi jaaataa bhaaayaa. Humein Khan Market ke lanes kee badbooo kee aadat hai..."

Of course, I did not have the heart to say that. Even if I did, who'd have understood my pain? No one else was from Delhi, after all.

While everyone else jumped in and started frolicking another prudish friend and I stayed aloof. A few minutes later, my conscience did not allow me to keep standing like a disgruntled "*Phoopha ji*" at a wedding. I

Wisdom From The Smiling Panda

decided to dip my feet in that sludgy water.

Sir gently said, I could guarantee you that you will not die if you enter.

Say Hello To Phobia

I started feeling as scared as I could ever remember feeling in my life. Gone were the South Delhi instincts. They were replaced by anxiety and a feeling of intense fear.

Now I have to tell you this. The water in the cave was perhaps only 8-9 feet deep. Technically, even if someone wanted to, they would not drown in it. I mean, unless someone pushed your head down and held you there. Fortunately, no one in our group showed homicidal tendencies, so murder was also out of the question.

I have never had any scary experiences with water, as far as my memory recalls.

Though I never learned to swim, I have never been averse to being around water. The fear I started experiencing was incredibly stunning to me. Perhaps some past life memory of drowning was activated.

Here walked one of the brightest brains I have had a chance to know, **Apoorva**.

As the fear surged through my body, no matter what my fellow batchmates said or even the words of encouragement from my teacher did not matter. I was experiencing phobias and fearing for my life.

I think I will never forget how Apoorva floated towards me, held my hands, and said, "It is alright. You will not drown. I will hold on to you, and we can swim across this cave. Trust me, I will not let go."

Boom!

Being a person struggling with phobias and the fear of dying, a surprising calmness seeped inside of me. Holding on to her hands, not only could I swim across the cave, but I could also notice how others were having a happy time, even if I could not reach that state. Heck, she even managed to convince me to take a full dip in the slu...water.

As we finally climbed out of the cave, I was relieved to be 'alive', but the impact of Apoorva's sincere energy and confidence-inducing words had certainly carved a special place in my bank of memories.

Impact Of Inspiration

A conscious and fortunate person who has been uplifted by another human can tell you how much of a difference that can make.

This little hike episode made me reflect on the often subtle and uplifting impact some humans' words, presence, and energy can have.

From a literal failure in Mathematics, I turned into a consistently high-scoring student thanks to the confidence and right coaching given by Verma sir.

I recall my early days in theatre, where despite being one of the most talented (humbly so) people, I could rarely express it for lack of confidence. My mentor's faith in my abilities inspired me to rock it on stage.

In the chapter calle"Power Of A Gaze", I have written about how a friend's mere gaze led me to win a debate competition in college.

More than anything or anyone else, **Bhagavan Shri Krishna's timeless and legendary words from the Bhagavad Gita** completely overhauled the quality of my life and continue to give meaning, purpose, and hope in the bleakest and most challenging of times.

Has a fellow being ever inspired you? (journal prompt)

Share your story with me if you feel like it. I'd love to hear if a coach, a mentor, or a teacher impacted your life positively.

Thank you for reading until the end of the piece. I hope this inspires some hope, inspiration, and joy.

On The Need To Feel Seen

A development in my life that I cherish is understanding and acknowledging the human need to feel seen. I take it as a significant thing as I observe its impact on human interpersonal relationships.

Whenever I find myself in my favourite cafe, the courtesy exuded towards me by some of the staff emboldens my belief in the merit of seeing people with eyes of respect.

One staff member recently confided in me how she feels pleased when I greet her using her name. Now that is something so basic that it defies logic that something as simple can make people happy! I could deduce, though, how much it means to an individual if they feel seen and heard.

A funny and ironic contrast is how people feel when they are left on "seen" on social media.

Personal Reflections

A few years back, some neighbours who shifted to the block where we live ended up connecting with even the former residents just because of their kind acknowledgement of people's presence. I have seen how my mother feels when even strangers greet her with warmth. A simple yet profound cue of how simple things matter so much.

I recall some of my visits to a childhood friend's home. On one occasion, his father took us on his scooter for an ice cream treat at *Mother Dairy*. This incident happened over fifteen years ago. Yet, I felt joy recalling it even as I was twisting in *Matsyendra Asana* this morning. I am no longer in touch with that friend, and it has been a long, long time since I saw the friend's father, yet his kind, smiling face is still firmly etched in my subconscious. I would have had innumerable ice creams since then, but none perhaps as remarkable as that because the kid me needed that.

I remember this technique of making people see was employed by one of my theatre teachers and colleagues. I noticed how she giving her time and energy to students (mainly after a successful stage show) and made people really happy. The way some people like yours truly felt obliged towards her for her attentiveness is all the compelling proof I can share to substantiate my point.

I can keep on writing more examples, like:

- That mentor whose sweet and kind voice itself can melt even the hardest heart.

- My maternal grandfather brought me 'Crackle' every evening when I visited him.

- That nurse 'Aunty' had such warmth and kindness in her eyes whenever she looked towards me.

- Or say in popular culture the indelible impact of a character like <u>Ted Lasso</u>.

Our Charity

I see all these people whose examples I quote as charitable individuals. We speak and give a lot of attention, for good measure, to the hunger pangs of the stomach. However, another essential hunger that needs acknowledgement and validation is the human need to feel seen and loved. No matter who you are, even if you're God, we are all looking to feel love. In the Vedic context, **Krishna** is seen as the Supreme God who is the embodiment of love. A divine entity who gives love and is only pleased by the offering of love.

Unfortunately, we often underplay the importance of this kind of charity. While the need to contribute via resources, money, food, and services is essential, there can be a solid case to address people's hunger for love and attention.

My personal game-changer is to learn about my own need to feel validated, seen, and heard. That makes it easier for me to recognise when the condition becomes a compulsive addiction that has the potential to manipulate or be manipulated by others. Additionally, it makes me reiterate the importance of bringing in self and divine love to keep my love tank full.

The idea of this kind of charity is an attempt to create a culture of respect and human dignity.

"There is more hunger for love and appreciation in this world than for bread." - Mother Teresa

Here's a question and reflection for you, dear reader:

What makes you feel seen? (Journal prompt.)

Reflect on the moments in your life when you feel acknowledged and valued. Share it with your loved ones or with me if you feel like it.

Thank you for reading until the end of the piece. If you liked what I wrote, do share your views. God bless you with a lot of self-validation, compassion, and love.

The Power Of Intent

"Be thankful for what you have now because the things you have right now are what you once wished for."

The above quote is something we all would have heard or read at some point in time, and today I could deeply appreciate the sentiment behind it. So often, we go through life oblivious to the fact that many things we once desired have been delivered by the universe.

I journal using an app called **Day One**, which I may have mentioned another time here if you're a regular here. I use a digital journal because, hey, there is no denying our reliance on our gadgets these days. Secondly, the benefit of a digital journal is privacy. Thirdly, it is about the little reminders that come in the form of "on this day last year".

Today my previous year's journal entry reminded me about:

- My unhealthy addiction to Moong Dal Barfi, which I used to gorge on like *Kumbhkaran* eating food after six months of sleep.
- A lack of discipline and direction in my personal health practice.
- A desire to get addicted to yoga.

My Yoga teacher's training was a few months away at this time last year. As I reflect back upon my state back then, what strikes me is how I had the right intentions to improve despite the challenges. There was a longing to be in a better state of being. One year on, a lot has changed by the absolute divine grace of spirit—Krishna, inspirational friends, and dedicated teachers.

If you listen to successful humans talk about their lives, you find a common thread : they setpositive intentions and have a sincere desire to improve. They would also tell you, especially those humans who have an active connection to the spirit, that 'how' the intention manifests is not as essential as setting an intention and surrendering.

The method they employ is:

- To see where there is a lack in their life.
- Set a positive desire, and intention for the same.
- Do their daily duties with gratitude.

- Do not worry about how the intention will fructify.
- Most importantly, have faith in the divine.

An idea that has really resonated with me is to set intentions and free yourself from the anxiety of their fulfilment. I find this idea in resonance with the teachings of **Bhagavan Shri Krishna** in the **Bhagavad Gita** and something that frees me from my ego and brings me peace.

I am not the controller, there are factors beyond my control, yet the universe is always helping each one if they are willing to attune to it.

As I observe how much my relationship with my body, cravings, food, and discipline have improved, I can authentically appreciate the power of setting positive intentions.

I implore you, dear reader, to reflect. What aspect of your life do you have an intense yearning to improve?

Is it your interpersonal relationship?

Finances?

Work?

Health?

A creative engagement?

What positive intention do you wish to set today? (Journal prompt.)

Write it down. Set a reminder for this time next year, and who knows? Life may positively surprise and overwhelm you.

Thank you for reading until the end of the piece. I hope this sparks ideas that bring inspiration and hope.

The Merits Of Having A Personal God

अर्जुन उवाच

एवं सततयुक्ता ये भक्तास्त्वां पर्युपासते ।

ये चाप्यक्षरमव्यक्तं तेषां के योगवित्तमाः ॥ १ ॥

BHAGAVAD GITA 12.1

Arjuna inquired: Which are considered to be more perfect, those who are always properly engaged in Your devotional service, or those who worship the impersonal Brahman, the unmanifested?

Arjuna asks this question right after the section in the Bhagavad Gita when Shri Krishna reveals His *universal form*. Arjuna could witness right there in the middle of the battlefield that His charming friend turned chariot driver contained the Universe within Himself. Arjuna is naturally in a confused state.

What will be better?

To contemplate and connect to what is manifest before him, or something impersonal?

क्लेशोऽधिकतरस्तेषामव्यक्तासक्तचेतसाम् ।
अव्यक्ता हि गतिर्दुःखं देहवद्भिरवाप्यते ॥ ५ ॥

BHAGAVAD GITA 12.5

"For those whose minds are attached to the unmanifested, impersonal feature of the Supreme, advancement is very troublesome. To make progress in that discipline is always difficult for those who are embodied."

In this beautiful verse from the Gita, **Shri Krishna** so logically points out that for the ones who are embodied, devotion to something formless is not easy.

I have been wondering lately how people can get so attached to deities and forms of divinity. Even books, symbols, gurus, or say, rituals. We see it more profoundly with religion, but it is also the case with pop culture. To give a few examples: **Batman** evokes more sentiments than comic books; **Manchester United** (toxically so in my case) evokes more emotions than the sport of Football; Sachin's retirement made me stop watching Cricket altogether.

I have been reading the Gita again, but this time my focus has been more on the impersonal angle, the

Advaita Vedanta (non-dualism) route. While most of the content spoken by the Mystical Shri Hari goes over my tiny brain, it still does not fail to astonish me. What it definitely made me think about is why there has been a need in human history to deify divinity or have a tangible form for worship. Reading the Gita from an *impersonal perspective* helps me appreciate the beauty of the above verse. Additionally, I can also appreciate why it is so easier to connect to some 'tangible' personal form like Krishna Himself.

Why A Deity

People who cannot understand or appreciate why there is a need for places of worship, deities, and symbols can do well to ruminate on B.G. 12.5 as quoted above.

Pay attention to the usage of the word **embodied**. It does not just mean the spirit that is right now expressing itself through the body; it also means one who cannot perceive that which is beyond the body.

We cannot explain the taste of a *rasgulla* to a person who has never tried it. However, one who has tasted something sweet previously can at least come to a state of imagination.

When the divine descends in the form of, say, Krishna (or, say, a master, a saint, or a prophet), it becomes so infinitely easy to connect with. The beautiful form, play, interactions, stories, and qualities of a personal form can so effortlessly attract our minds and hearts towards divinity. The advantage a personal form brings is immense!

The first step of approaching the divine is usually out of fear, awe, or some need. That is a good start but it is definitely not first class. A higher step can be to humanise the relationship with God.

In **Vaishnav tradition**, there are primarily five ways, or more specifically, *rasas,* as they are called in Sanskrit, of connecting with God:

- **Shant ras**: Silent contemplation on God. Usually in the form of Lord **Narayana** (Vishnu). We find similar paths preached in other religions as well. Here God is treated with awe and reverence.

- **Dasya ras**: One now has a more personal connection. One connects to the Lord as a servant. The most famous example is **Shri Hanuman** from Ramayana.

- **Sakhya ras**: Here the mood is that of a friend, and clearly there is greater level of intimacy. Think of **Arjuna, Sugriva, or Vibhishan** from the epics.

- **Vatsalya ras**: Here one thinks of themselves as a parent of the divine. The divine is seen as dependent and the level of intimacy and love is unmatched. We all know how legendary is the love between **Mother Yasoda** and Baby Krishna.

- **Madhurya ras**: The mood here is that of a lover. One considers God their beloved, and all other rasas find expression here. The **Gopis of Vrindavan** is the prime example of this mood.

The reason I gave the above examples is to exemplify how these paths have been created to facilitate an easier route towards the divine.

The path of knowledge, or **Jnana yoga,** may not be everyone's cup of tea. It is not easy at all to engage your intellect in trying to understand that which is beyond the intellect itself.

The path of **ashtanga yoga** and its eight limbs are practically impossible to achieve for 90% of the populace in the modern era—I say that with some conviction after studying about the eight limbs during my yoga teacher training.

The path of devotion, or love, is the easiest and most practical. One can use practically all human emotions to connect with the divine. One can use even ordinary day-to-day activities to connect to God and divinise our humanity. I have learned recently that for this reason, even students of Advaita Vedanta are advised to first start with the **12th chapter of the Gita,** which directly deals with the path of divine love. Even **Shri Aadi Shankaracharya,** the proponent of **non-dualism** at the end of His human adventure, advised devotion to Shri Krishna (refer to Bhaja Govindam) as a sure shot way of rising above the material life!

God is not an idea or a concept that can be explained. God is not even an object that can be defined. God is ultimately an experience, as explained by the wise ones. A personal form makes it so much easier to get a glimpse of the experience.

Wishing you the best on your life journey,

Journal Prompt: What is your personal idea about God and divinity? Is there any spiritual icon that piques your interest or inspires you?

Physical Fitness And Yogic Lifestyle

I had a happy and profound realization that just as it is wise to travel light on a journey, it can also be easier to navigate through life if you are carrying less weight on your body and mind.

My yoga teacher's training (@ <u>govardhan school of yoga</u>) was phenomenal for my personal life. I learned about an evolved and healthier lifestyle. A nice side effect was burning unnecessary fat. Now, losing fat like sex is something that almost everyone desires, but not everyone gets to have. And if someone gets either of the two, people tend to get curious, how did you manage to do it? And inevitably, the people who get it either end up acting smug or saying, "No big deal."

Nope, both happen to be big deals!

Many acquaintances and friends asked about how the

weight loss journey happened. When an old school friend said she'd be willing to read about the process, I decided to write a piece on some of the most important things I learned about health during my yoga teacher's training. So thank you for prompting and inspiring me to share this.

Now let me put out a **caveat** before you delve further into the blog. This is not 'professional' advice. It is an informal sharing intended to be of help to the readers and friends. If you are serious about any health goal, please seek the guidance of a coach, consultant, or teacher. Frankly, I am still in the process of learning more about physical and mental wellness. I have humbly put forth ideas that have worked for my body.

Here's also an honest confession: losing fat or weight wasn't the goal when I went for my yoga teacher's training program; it just happened to be a nice byproduct for which I am sincerely grateful. So as you read along and have a particular fitness goal, I will share a humble realization:

It is better not to think much about the end goal. Instead, it would be best if we could wellness a lifestyle. Every other little or big fitness goal follows.

At the yoga school, all students followed what is known as **Dincharya** in yogic/Ayurvedic texts.

What it constitutes is the following:

1. Waking up before or around sunrise. It wasn't mandatory, but I followed it, and I have never felt

happier, or healthier in my body or mind. What it also meant was that to ensure consistent early rising, an early bedtime was compulsory.

2. We had two separate classic **hatha yoga and asana** classes, AM and PM. Both constituted around two hours or more of asana practise. We had an off day once a week, but twice within a month, on our off days, we went hiking in the mountains. Yep, you got it; good, solid work on the physical body.

3. The **food** served was sattvik vegetarian, which not only nourishes the body but also helps the mind and the energies come to a level of receptivity to understand higher philosophy and ways of living. In Bharat, since ancient times, we are told,

"जैसा खाओगे अन्न वैसा होगा मन।"

This means that what you eat has an impact on your mind and consciousness.

I will not act like a bigot and preach to you the morality of staying off non-vegetarian food and intoxicants here.

If you like indulging in them, that's completely alright. You should be aware of what to eat and how much.

The idea is to eat in moderation and know how much to put in the body.

If you have no spiritual aspiration, eating non-vegetarian food, drinking alcohol, or doing drugs is fine as long as you know your limit. Yes, you read that right. Whatever makes you happy.

And on that note, if you want to still indulge in spiritual practices while enjoying sensual pleasures, the best path is **mantra meditation** on the name of **Shri Krishna**. That will help you overcome anything that inhibits your growth—material or spiritual.

Another **important note on food** is that the biggest meal of the day is to be had between 10 a.m. and 12 p.m., when the Sun is supposed to assist you in firing up your digestion and the second before sunset, around 6-7 p.m. Or ideally, within an hour of sunset. One may take warm milk before bedtime. In the afternoon, one may indulge in a light, healthy snack.

One of my teachers shared a fascinating idea about food that was previously unknown to me. He said the first burp is an indication that the stomach is full. The second is the body pleading with you to stop, and so on. In an earlier meditation class I attended years back, a teacher shared that the ideal quantity of food should be as much as can be contained in your palms!

4. The game-changer for me personally was the elimination of white sugar. Prior to myyogic education, I had never contemplated or even considered quitting processed sugar. Neither was I honestly aware of the adverse effects it can have. Sweets of any kind were my drug, as my friend, Sarvesh, once pointed out when he saw me gorge on *gulab jamuns* one after another at a friend's wedding. No wonder I started looking like a Gulab Jamun before yoga!

Our yoga teacher was strict about the no-sugar rule, and now I'm thankful to him for the same.

Seek A Higher Taste

In the **Bhagavad Gita**, Verse 59 of the second chapter, Bhagavan **Krishna** makes this genius statement:

विषया विनिवर्तन्ते निराहारस्य देहिनः।

रसवर्जं रसोऽप्यस्य परं दृष्ट्वा निवर्तते ॥

In the plain English language, this can be explained as meaning that without experiencing a higher taste, one cannot simply disengage from sensual pleasures.

My yoga teacher said to me that for him, it's been 17 years practising yoga, and still, his mind tries to trick him out of doing his daily workout/yoga regime! Working on the body is a challenge each day.

But, as Shri Hari (another name for Krishna) explains, when you do gain a higher taste (in our case, some positive changes in your body), you are much more equipped to handle the tribulations of the mind.

I still love sweets. I still indulge in them. However, I prefer homemade sweets sans processed sugar to the ones available on the market. I also ensure I check the ingredients label on any food item I am buying. If the food item is simply loaded with sugar, it is better to avoid it. However, after a few months of practice, you will reach an understanding of what is good for your body. In time, you can also easily be able to eat your favourite food items in moderation and also maintain a healthy body.

The Mind Will Never Make It Easy

I'll tell you, as my yoga teacher pointed out, it is still not easy to roll out the yoga mat in the morning. I have resigned myself to the fact that it might never be easy, but I have to do it anyway. Most importantly, I love the progress that has come from investing a lot of time, money, and effort more than sweets or mind protests at doing the practice. That is the higher taste!

I also try to keep tricking the mind by mixing and matching the physical practices. Combining yoga with running and resistance band training works like a blessing. I would implore you as well to have a few options handy.

A typical conversation between the mind and intelligence in the morning happens as follows:

Mind: We did not get much sleep last night. Better to skip yoga right now. We can always do it in the evening.

Intelligence: What if I am not free on time from work in the evening?

Mind: Oh, we will. You need to respect the body as well.

Intelligence: Doing yoga practise is respecting the body, dodo. And if we do our routine now, we can enjoy our free time in the evening.

Mind: Uhhh...Shall we just do one part of the practice followed by pranayama?

Intelligence: Sure, why not. Only 5-10 minutes...

One teacher at the yoga school told me, "**No matter how busy you are, give yourself just five minutes on the mat**." That is a genius formula. Those five minutes usually turn into more than that. Trust me on this: there are a few things that feel as good as committing time for your body and mind's well-being. Following through with personal commitments gives one a profound sense of confidence and joy. A book suggestion that can help you create good habits that stick is **"Atomic Habits" by James Clear.**

The Boon of Technology

I'll conclude by sharing a personal hack that has surprisingly been incredibly helpful for me—my smartwatch. By setting my daily move, exercise and stand goals, I check my progress and commitment to the body. I'll be level with you on this; the congratulatory message on hitting all these goals is a positive boost! I may not have been as consistent had these daily reminders not popped up on the watch.

Whether we agree or not, **we all crave affirmations and rewards**.

Our brain craves rewards for the work we put in. When that doesn't come, it isn't easy to stay motivated.

So, having a fitness device/smartwatch can also be really handy in our fitness journey.

I hope the post inspires you to commit more time to your physical body. It took me thirty years to realize that one cannot escape the daily hard or happy work on the body if one has to remain healthy. There are no shortcuts or cheat codes. It is never too late to begin.

Just make sure you seek help. It can be arduous to go alone on such a journey. Having a good trainer or coach can be a game-changer. I have used the example of yoga, which worked for me. Maybe for you, it can be gymming, running, or something else.

Thank you for reading this. If this helps you, please

pray that I remain committed to the path of a yogic lifestyle.

Journal Prompt: What do you do to keep yourself physically active? How can you add to your personal fitness?

On Defining Purpose

So many people who have succumbed lately have left behind grieving family and friends. In general, one can notice that whenever someone passes on, we find people who had an active connection to the dead person suffering. This leads me to contemplate the importance of individuals and their purposes.

An issue that I find plaguing many millennials is finding their purpose. So much so that they can enrol in expensive courses, programs, coaching, and whatnot just to find their hallowed purpose. Pegged on by motivational speakers, cinema, and other mass media, many feel their lives are meaningless if they fail to find their purpose. Curiously, for most, finding their purpose means:

- rebelling against the world

- becoming famous
- becoming rich
- having lots of followers
- travelling (many times for the sake of their Instagram art gallery), etc.
- making a 'dent' in the Universe

There is nothing wrong with any of the above, of course. These are all good things to aim for if the *heart and conscious action* drive one towards them.

Coming back again to the ones who have left their mortal coils. You will find that most who have died did not have much of a following or a social circle. They perhaps only had a close-knit circle of friends and family. Their loss, though, haunts their loved ones as much as a loss of a cherished public figure. In a perverted sense of defining purpose, one may say that many have gone have failed to discover their purpose.

But is it really so?

When we lose someone close to us to the humbling phenomenon of death, our thoughts usually go towards the happy moments that consciousness helped us experience. We lament that loss because of the importance and impact that consciousness in a human (or animal) form had on your system. We remember the moments of love, of giving, and of sharing that made us feel alive.

What does that entail?

Purpose is kind of fulfilled.

It is sad that in mass media and this day and age, when there is an apparent encouragement to project what you are not, there is a lot of dissatisfaction, especially amongst the urban population, about a lack of purpose.

The purpose is not necessarily about the number of people reached or impacted. The purpose is about doing something with an intention to be helpful, of service and with a bit of heart.

In doing so, even ordinary, mundane activities become purposeful and impactful.

I'm sure you have heard of the story of a man who encounters three individuals on a construction site.

Once, a gentleman sees a few people working on a construction site. He asks the first person, "What are you doing here, sir?"

The man replies, "Can't you see where we are and what I'm doing?" (basically, this guy was like, *Raasta naap, chaccha, bakaiti ka time nahi?*)

The gentleman asked the second person working on the site the same question. He replied, "We are working on some building, sir. I don't care about the details. I just do my work so I can get paid."

When the gentleman asks the third person working on the site, he replies happily, "Sir, we're working to build a beautiful temple. I'm so happy I got a chance to be a part of this project."

The story above is significant because it talks about the same work providing a different meaning to different people depending on the attitude they bring to it.

The first guy was "FML", or "Monday vibe."

The second was like, "You've got to do what you must do.

The third found meaning in what he was doing and felt joyous.

An idea that I dare put forth is that perhaps your work is not your purpose. In other words, the career that pays you is not your purpose, but you may need to be engaged in it anyway. Maybe your purpose is just to mow the lawn, water the plants, bring a glass of water for a family member, take care of your animal, pick up litter off the street and drop it in the trash can, or simply give a kind smile to a fellow human, and so forth. It is in these seemingly small things that purpose can manifest.

Let me conclude by sharing an incident when I felt purposeful.

Back when I was doing my yoga teacher's training at Govardhan Eco Village, almost every evening I went to take darshan of **Shri Giriraj Govardhan** (a manifestation of Shri **Krishna**). While circumambulating the embodiment of the Lord, I saw a plastic water bottle on the trail. My immediate response was irritation mixed with anger at the lack of civic sense of some people in the country. My mind even thought of some really *'sweet and gentle'* words that are the hallmark of a Delhi guy (think of **Virat Kohli** on a Cricket field). But, blame it on the conditioning of the spiritual atmosphere and Shri Krishna, I uncharacteristically picked it up and dropped it in the trash basket. This entire exercise somehow made me feel good.

Why?

Because I felt it was useful to contribute by picking up the bottle, which would have been picked up anyway by the diligent staff at the eco-village who're so particular about cleanliness. Maybe some other guest or student would have done it sans any irritability like mine. But, the fact that I could be used and inspired for that little act when no one was around to pat my back or praise me was humbling.

That is how purpose can work. It may be doing the most insignificant thing that someone else will do anyway. But God gave you a chance to be of use and service. And when one can program their mind like that, boom! Every day of life becomes meaningful, purposeful, and a reason to be grateful.

Do you have a story to share?

When did you feel purposeful in your life?

I'd be pleased to read, hear, and know about your experiences and thoughts.

You will feel purposeful if this resonates with you,

Let Fear Find You And Do Not Be Afraid

In the movie The **Dark Knight Rises**, Bruce has failed a few times trying to escape the pit where he is imprisoned to languish and die. When an older prisoner sees him fall yet again in his efforts to escape, he offers some words of wisdom.

"You do not fear death. You think it makes you strong?

It makes you weak.

How can you move faster than possible, fight longer than possible without the most powerful impulse of the spirit?

The fear of death."

The Dark Knight Rises

Unimaginably horrific scenes are on display in the nation as of now (Written during the second wave of the COVID pandemic in India, during which countless human beings lost their lives). It seems as if we shifted into some alternate reality within the space of a few weeks. In what seemed like an emergence from the dystopian times of 2020, we find ourselves in a much scarier scenario.

There are many ifs and buts, blame, frustration, anger, and pain, and that too for good measure. For the ones who have had to struggle to get a basic human need of healthcare met and have seen a family member succumb to the virus in times when one cannot even get to say a proper goodbye, all this has been scarring.

So, yes. All of it should make us fearful.

We were lost in the haze and maze of modern life. Suddenly, life and its fragility are magnified. It's a kind of daily reminder no one asked for. Nature has its way of signalling that the time is nigh for one to shed the body, i.e., old age. But, the virus is taking people of all ages.

No distinction.

No notification.

We are all, in a way, hanging on for dear life. You do not know when or how the virus will strike. And even if, by the grace of God, you remain safe, what about the people you love and care about?

Stay Alive

If you're reading this, you're still safe. You're still around. You're still getting to rejoice in this magical, precious gift called life. No matter how hard it seems, life is still worth fighting for. Life is worth living. I hope you agree.

I was speaking to a few friends recently. I mentioned how even if **Bhagavan Krishna** comes and offers me His eternal abode with a guarantee of bliss and joy, would I be willing to let go of my attachment to my body and situations? Even in the current scenario?

Honestly, not really.

I may believe and read up on all the scriptures and find solace in a divine figure like Bhagavan Krishna, and I will still hold my life dear. When this is the state of the ones like me who believe in the afterlife, rebirth, and so on, what to imagine for those who think this is the only one life, one chance!

What do we do now, though?

People have died. We can cry, lament, and drive ourselves mad over these things, but the harsh, fierce truth is that the ones who have died aren't returning.

The Way Forward

Returning to our Batman analogy, when that old prisoner suggested Bruce find fear, was it to demoralise him?

To somehow inculcate a cynical ideology into him?

Nope.

The prisoner wanted Bruce to use fear as an impulse to increase his will to survive. To remind him that death is certain anyway, and there is nothing glorious in dying in a pathetic condition without trying all possible means to live and survive!

So, what do we do?

We fight.

We strengthen ourselves.

We do our best to ensure we do not become carriers of the virus and do not burden the system any further.

You may ask, "Kushagra, if you have any ideas, suggestions, inputs, or insights?"

Let me present some steps I undertake to keep myself sane and uplifted and find my version of fear of death and love for living. I call it the *Pandemic Dharma* (however, it's good to keep using it even after coming out of the pandemic).

1. **Engage in some conscious breathing, breathwork, and pranayama practises.**

I use my post to remind us yet again of the timeless practise of Pranayama.

Don't hesitate, don't delay;, just for the sake of survival, do it. When we survive the pandemic, we'll thank ourselves for choosing a holistic practise such as pranayama.

To help out, I suggest three practices (to be done in the mentioned order) for the best effect:

- Bhastrika/Kalapabhati (please check their contra-indications in case you have some medical conditions such as high BP, etc.)
- Anulom Vilom
- Bhramari

My additional two cents is that you should get a guide or teacher to learn it from.

2. Use Ayurvedic herbs

Giloy, **Neem**, **Turmeric** (mixed with black pepper is even better), **Tulsi** (Holy Basil)—Taking these herbs early in the morning on an empty stomach condition can boost your immunity tremendously. Safe and effective. I say this with authoritative experience. We also must be adding multivitamins and supplements like zinc, vitamin C, and vitamin D.

3. Engage in some daily movement

Walk, run, hop, skip, jump, cycle, or, my pick, do yoga. Just move—minimum 30 minutes. If you can give an hour to the body, oh boy, your body will be so thankful, and your experience of living in it will be so rewarding. Take it from me—someone who has spent a decade of his life trying to find shortcuts and cheat codes to health, there are none. You have to invest time in your body. And speaking of the body, it brings us to point four.

4. Invest time in meditation (mind)

We need to ensure the mind remains healthy, especially now. Meditation of any form can help you you move from a reactive state to a state of conscious response.

Guided meditations are fantastic, to begin with. To find a teacher or read a book. Or use a piece of nice calming music (my suggestion is that you use **binaural beats**), get comfortable, use some deep breathing exercises and use your imagination productively. Visualise a healthy and happy you. That'll take care of your fear.

A little word of a caveat: *It takes time.* Be patient. Don't expect miraculous changes the first day you engage in meditative practice. It can even take years, honestly. I'll not offer any fake advertisements for meditation. But, if you're sincere and committed, you will see positive changes soon, so much so that they become a part of a brand-new and refined you!

5. Prayers

There's a saying that one is an atheist only until the plane starts falling. *I say even the ones pretending to be theistic are atheists until the plane of their lives, dreams, and plans starts crashing.*

I have spent sixteen (and counting) years reading and experimenting with spiritual practices. My life has transformed. It sort of feels it has felt like a new life since my introduction to **Shri Krishna**.

But, upon honest reflection and contemplation, I realize I chose to be selective, and thrifty in applying spiritual wisdom and tools. The virus, finding the fear of death, and awakening to the reality of mortality have me thinking that for the ones who survive, the virus can be a tremendous teacher to make lifestyle shifts. Heck, if we, the ones who survive (Amen), do not make lifestyle shifts, then it'll be a missed opportunity.

Prayer connects you to the divine that is within. You discover the potential power lying latent. You find out the gift that the divine has offered for us to choose to connect to it.

Prayer is not a demand for fulfilling your bucket list but an affirmation of love and belonging to something indestructible.

If you are a newbie, do not worry. Our ancestors have blessed us abundantly. Some powerful chants can not just shift reality for you but also put you on a course for liberation. Pick a chant or mantra and keep chanting as long as you're in a wakeful state, no matter what you're doing. Keep chanting internally while you eat, sleep, mate, wash, brush, watch TV, scroll your social media feed, etc. Of course, you should also devote focused time to chanting.

How to pick a chant?

You experiment.

Be a spiritual scientist. Use the chants, which are just powerful sound vibrations, to see which one you resonate with, and then keep chanting.

My suggestions?

- Om Namo Bhagavate Vasudevaye
- Om Namo Narayanaya
- Om Namah Shivaaye
- Hare Krishna Mahamantra (Hare Krishna, Hare Krishna, Krishna Krishna Hare Hare. Hare Ram, Hare Ram, Ram Ram, Hare Hare)

Do it consciously for even ten minutes every day and see the change. This form of meditation can fetch miraculous results if one is committed.

If you wish to read more ideas pertaining to the power of chanting mantras, you can refer to the chapter, "Higher Taste And Higher Purpose".

6. Read The Bhagavad Gita

Even when I'm using divinatory tools like **oracle/angel cards** for friends or clients, I refrain from making predictions.

But, I'm still going to stick my neck out and make a prediction that I hope comes true:

Never again are we going to face such tumultuous

times as a species in the coming century? Fingers crossed, Om Tat Sat, Inshallah, and all that.

Now that we are here and surviving:

Please Make Use Of The Fear!

Please Read The Bhagavad Gita!

If you were to ask me what should be the two primary takeaways for anyone who reads this post, then my pick would be points 1 and 6, i.e., pranayama and reading Gita. Both of these should be enough for a healthy person to manage fear and boost inner strength.

When I see the pain in people's hearts at the tragic loss of lives, I wonder how much of a missed opportunity it is on the part of this land that the teachings of the Gita are not propagated.

The words of **Krishna** will not alleviate the pain, but they certainly act as a soothing balm for the miseries and challenges we encounter as we are alive. If read with devotion, they also empower you to become fearless and evolved.

If you do read it, please send a blessing and prayer my way as well. Hopefully, even I can integrate some Gita into my daily life.

On that note, seek good company, talk to positive people, read uplifting books, and watch good content on TV. All such things have a tremendous impact on our mental well-being as well.

7. Gratitude

If death does have to come, what will be better, to die miserably or to die with gratitude?

I like to think the latter is a better option.

The latter is not just a better option for dying but also for living.

The daily practise of gratitude can help alleviate the anxiety associated with the adverse events we perceive. Within a few weeks, we can rewire our subconscious to start looking for opportunities rather than obstacles.

Every day, pick three things you're thankful for in the morning and before going to bed. You can do more, for sure. Start with three, though.

Reflect upon the already beautiful moments you have experienced in life rather than stressing about what may be and allowing the monkey mind to conjure horrific scenarios, most of which (thankfully!) will never come to pass.

Thank you so much for reading through until the end of the post. I hope, pray, and wish that the post brings you some upliftment and joy in our testing times. God bless you and keep living. I, too, hope to come back with another chapter or another book.

P. S. In the movie **Batman Begins** (the first part of the Dark Knight Trilogy), when Bruce's father is shot in the alley by a mugger, his father's last words to him are, Bruce, don't be afraid.

So, hey, Bruce (reader), don't be afraid.

Journal Prompt: What was your biggest lesson from the pandemic?

Reflections On Slowing Down

What does the phrase 'slow down' mean to you? (Journal prompt.)

We've all heard of "slowing down" a lot this year (written in 2020), haven't we?

Perhaps a bit too much. More than we'd have liked anyway.

The pandemic seems unending, even with the uplifting news of vaccine(s) ready for rollout.

At the beginning of the pandemic, slowing down perhaps meant restrictions on travel, meet-ups, shopping, venturing out for recreation, etc. As we approach the end of an infamous year as conscious beings, we must ask ourselves what exactly this enforced slowdown brought us.

Has it all been gloom and doom?

OR

Have we emerged stronger (both internally and externally) after surviving thus far?

As I write this, I wonder why anyone would want to slow down by choice?!

Life's a race, right?

Right from conception in the mother's womb, we're supposed to be running towards the grave. Often, without purpose or meaning; lacking any direction, yet always having the certainty that we're all heading for the same destination (death).

I think of all the happy times in my life and realize they all went by so quickly. At least what I feel were happy moments in retrospect. I doubt if I was enlightened enough to recognise and relish those moments as blessings and be immensely grateful. If we look at life from this perspective, we realize it is relatively brief and uncertain.

If we go by the Western and Abrahamic schools of thought, then you just have one life and one shot at fulfilment. After that, it's either eternal obscurity, enjoyment, or damnation. Well, no wonder; the ideas emerging from the West have taught us to be in a rush.

When we're overwhelmed with life, our mortal bodies, emotions, or dealings with others are usually reasons our well-wishers advise us to relax and slow down.

When too many accidents are robbing people of their lives the government comes out with warnings of 'speed thrills but kills'.

I think our our "body's government"—the soul—also comes out with such warnings in the form of anxiety, depression, confusion, disease, and so forth. That's when we need to check in with ourselves and see how to serve ourselves best.

I have personally realized lately that I have been someone who's been in a hurry for some reason. My friend Aditi pointed out how I spoke fast while conversing. It was pointed out a few others previously when I worked in theatre. My saving grace was the diction; otherwise, the words would have felt muddled up. I'd like to think the same about going through life; *if we're too much in a hurry, events can feel muddled up.*

There were many other areas where I thought I had always been in a rush. I do feel 'experienced' enough to share some of my personally realized benefits of slowing down in different areas of life.

- Safer vehicular drives
- Better decision making
- Better digestion due to mindful chewing of food
- Savouring food items
- Better running (more on that in a future blog post)
- Better writing

- Better spiritual साधना (practice)
- Better conversation flow

I'd like to leave you with some solid wisdom shared by **Sadhguru** in one of his disciples' gatherings. I'll humbly paraphrase what I heard in my words and understanding.

"Slowing down should mean slowing down the chatter of the mind. Slowing down the breaths (via yoga), words that come out of your mouth...your activities in the world."

Power Of Repetition

On the back of the festival of lights, I have been wondering how rituals and routines play such an integral role in the lives of us human beings. It is not that we do anything too different, yet the same sort of routine brings about a sense of celebration and joy.

Sometime back, a friend remarked that most of the self-help spiritual books get repetitive after a while; essentially, they speak about similar concepts, albeit the presentations may differ. Her observation may or may not hold but, it is essential to ride over the 'boredom' (if I may term it so) that repetition may bring. The reason is those useful concepts when repeated again and again find a sanctuary in our hearts and minds. They, in turn, lead to growth and well-being.

Why Repeat

Some studies claim that if we learn something new, most of it (there is some estimated percentage) gets lost from our conscious mind within 48 hours! This claim is verifiable, for if I were to ask you what you had for breakfast a few weeks ago, not many of you would be able to recall. Unless, of course, you follow a set breakfast *ritual*.

The mind's ability to absorb things that it intends to be useful for our functioning is quite an incredible gift. One can consciously use it to our advantage. I talk about this concept in a podcast episode I recorded a while back. Look for "Programming The Mind For Desirable Experiences'" on Wisdom From The Smiling Panda Podcast.

We understand through the study of the human brain that something becomes a long-term memory in either of the two cases:

- There is some *emotional experience* attached to the learning/event, or
- Through repetition

It is not always possible to ensure we have a strong emotional experience associated with learning. But, one can always take the repetition route to ensure we can hold on to what we learn.

What To Repeat

You've got to choose where in life you wish to grow.

What is it that needs your mind's attention?

Learning which new information adds to the quality of your life?

I pick spiritual knowledge as something that needs constant reinforcement in my life. I was sharing this with a dear friend lately that even though I did a proper systematic study of the **Bhagavad Gita** at the beginning of the year, as I go through it again, I find newer realizations. Many things seem to go over the head as well—the things I thought I had grasped! To give you another example, the great epic **Ramayana** is something I have been hearing and reading since childhood. Still, as recently as last week, I gained a new dimension in understanding some of the key concepts of the story.

I find a lot of value in being able to repeat spiritual concepts. They help me evolve at the various stages of my life whenever I take their shelter.

The same goes for books aimed to self-help as well. Usually, when we read such books, our minds are exposed to new ideas, all of which may not apply to our current scenario of life. As one reads them, one may pick one idea (or several) that appeals to us and try to work with it for some time. Later, we can gather more or ignore what does not apply to us.

I have realized that so often I have only just paced through many personal development books and content. Had I done that with only a handful of such books, I wouldn't have managed to find the kind of value I have throughout my adult life. I categorise my former self as someone who read but didn't prioritise applying. Even then, I can humbly state that I have managed to improve. Because, as I said, if we keep exposing ourselves to an idea (hopefully a positive, uplifting one), we can find that the idea propels us towards growth.

Tackling Boredom

In his groundbreaking debut book, "Atomic Habits", **James Clear** gives a beautiful insight into champion athletes. In the book, James mentions that champions aren't the ones who always enjoy following routines. Champions are those who stick to the routine despite the boredom (I paraphrased what my mind grasped from the reading I did at the beginning of the year).

When we begin something new, it is usually exciting; however, we gain only when we have the mental fortitude to repeat it. This holds especially true for meditation, Japa, or even activities like exercise, eating healthy, sleeping early, etc.

I leave you with a question to contemplate, dear reader:

What needs repetition in your life? How do you stand to gain from it?

God bless you with joy and growth.

Source Lagwa Lo!

Once a disciple of the **Bhaktivedanta Swami Prabhupāda** asked him, "How can one get out of the clutches of Maya (duality)?"

Swamiji said, "It's impossible."

The disciple was stunned!

Impossible?!

He thought that perhaps I did not address my question correctly. Let me ask again on another occasion by rephrasing it.

Next time he asked, "Prabhupāda, I was wondering that there is so much suffering and agony in the conditioned state for the living entity; can there be a way to go beyond it?"

Once again, Swamiji said, "It is impossible."

The disciple, who was a sincere seeker, was disheartened again. If going beyond the conditionings of life is impossible, then why do we even engage in spiritual (or even material) activities?

The disciple wanted to give his question another try. His question was sincere and came from a desire to grow and learn. He knew that if his spiritual master will provided the same answer, it would shatter him.

He asked Prabhupāda once again, "Master, is it really impossible to go beyond this dual nature of life?"

This time, once again, the same answer was given, and the master started walking away. The disciple was despondent.

However, as Prabhupāda was walking away, he suddenly stopped. Turning to his disciple with a smile, he said, "It is impossible, but if Govind *(Krishna) sanctions, you can easily overcome anything.*"

A Smart Approach

Have you ever been to a place where the dog is less of a pet and more of a beast ready to pounce, not to give and receive affection but to give bites and receive a part of your flesh?

Well, I have.

When I encountered such a dog, I realized that, just like people, there are good dogs and bad dogs.

Anyway, have you also noticed that, no matter how violent an animal may be, if you approach the master, he will put the animal in check?

One can apply a similar approach to the energy (Duality) and source (God).

Going Beyond Frustrations

Frustrations invariably arise when we put in intense efforts for something, and it doesn't yield. In other words, we usually act with an endeavour in mind, but it doesn't always go according to plan.

However, if we observe life closely, we realize we are just a part of the cycle of life. The result of an actions but also is the cumulative combination of not only our action but specific determinants beyond our control.

For instance, in another era of this world when we had Marvel movies released in cinema halls, I wanted to watch **End Game**, first day, first show. I couldn't. I was ready to pay 1500-2000 bucks, get the best seats at the best cinema but, no. Others were ahead in line, perhaps alert, perhaps luckier, probably with some *'jugaad'*!

The point being if we only ever rely solely on our efforts in life, frustration and disappointment will be inevitable.

It is worth reflecting on how we as a society have ended up judging (ourselves mostly) by asking for help as weak. I'm starting to now look upon it as a sign of intelligence.

In the story above, **Swami Prabhupāda** subtly and smartly pointed out to his disciple that nothing is impossible with grace.

If we were to just go within—in our minds and hearts—and ruminate upon the miracles that we keep witnessing in our day-to-day lives, we would be easily able to appreciate and tap into that grace of the source. Manifestations are often as easy as the nails that grow on your fingers, the hair that grows on one's head (and other unwanted places), the trees that arise from tiny little seeds, the miraculous process of birth on the planet, and so forth.

Name it what you want- source, the field of intention, God, power, etc.—yet the idea is the same, the effect universal.

We want to live a life that enables us to experience freedom and peace. When we know that there is a power that may be unseen but can be felt and experienced with some serious reflection, worries dissipate like Millenial's savings!

When You Have A Backup

When, in the 1999 Cricket World Cup, **Saurav Ganguly and Rahul Dravid** smashed the Sri Lankan bowlers all around the stadium, an elder said to me, "They could only score so many runs because they knew **Sachin** was still in the dressing room and ready to come and bat if needed. They played without fear!"

While the gentleman was a huge Sachin fan, the point he was trying to make was that people can do extraordinary things when they have assurance of backing.

Players play better when backed by the manager, employee performance gets better with incentives and encouragement; and so on.

When we, while going through our life journey, attach ourselves to the idea that the **Universe** is a friendly source that only wants to help, life becomes easier to navigate.

You may ask how to do that, Kushagra?

Well, a mere intention is enough.

Or

Rather than directing the question to any mortal, you direct the question to the universe itself!

I leave you with a couple of questions for contemplation:

What do you think is impossible in your life right now?

What would you like help with?

Thank you so much for taking the time to read this piece.

God bless you with vibrant health and joy.

A Bit On Faith

A while back, I assisted in a guided meditation for a group of people on creating a consciousness of abundance. In the meditation, we imagined ourselves standing on an ocean shore and soaking in the abundance that is available from the universe to each of us. This exercise is fascinating because it goes on to show how each one of us accepts blessings from the universe as per our *capacity to receive them.*

I found it intriguing how each one of us who was involved in the exercise had our way of collecting the richness that the universe gave away. Some collected it in the palm of their hands, some in their arms, and some had buckets!

I mainly wanted to stress the point that there is no need for competition or to be a part of any 'rat race'. I mean, why be part of one when the supreme consciousness has not made you a rat? We saw how each person who was at the shore collecting their share of abundance didn't affect the other person's share at all.

It is so imperative to drill into this consciousness in our day and time. How we perceive the world hugely impacts the kind of experience we get to have here.

What are your ideas about life?

Do you believe you deserve the richness and fullness of life?

Do you think that one gets rich only by unfair means or by stepping upon another?

In my podcast episode, 'How to Hoodwink Destiny' (on Wisdom From The Smiling Panda Podcast, available on Spotify, Apple Podcasts, I narrated the story of a couple who manage to lead an abundant life despite having a प्रारब्ध or 'kismet' of serving horses.

As soon as we bring ourselves to the consciousness that we are more than just this body and focus on crafting a connection with Spirit, the easier life becomes. In that state, we often find a space for miracles, magical manifestations, healings, ideas, abundance, etc.

I remember wanting to begin writing seriously for many years. However, I was hesitant and fearful.

Why?

Because I didn't know where and how I would find

ideas to churn out a blog a week.

I had previously written on **Medium** and for an e-magazine once in a while. That had not required any formal commitment. To embark on a weekly blog meant to get more serious about writing. I wasn't sure if I was up to it.

However, this brilliant idea struck me: I do not have to write as much as I have to force a breath or grow nails. If **Krishna** (Spirit) wants me to create something, the idea will be supplied.

It's funny because even when I wrote this, I felt I was out of any significant ideas to structure a piece together for a write-up. Yet here I am!

I am amazed at how Spirit has helped me in every step of the process, even when I had doubts.

प्रकृतेःक्रियमाणानि गुणैःकर्माणि सर्वशः ।

अहङ्कारविमूढात्मा कर्ताहमिति मन्यते ॥ २७ ॥

Bhagavad Gita, 3.27

Bhagavan Krishna advises in the **Bhagavad Gita** that, under the influence of our false ego, we tend to consider ourselves the sole cause of our actions. There are always so many more forces involved in each action that we perform than just our will and effort.

Faith is the magical formula that makes things happen. Every apparent wrong is corrected; every challenge leads the way to opportunity.

In the **Ramayana,** when **Bhagavan Ramachandra** leads

his monkey and bear army to the ocean shore without any concrete plan on how to cross it, one monkey puts it brilliantly,

"The one who helps souls cross the ocean of birth and death will surely help us cross this ocean."

Above is a classic example of having faith in the face of overwhelming challenges.

I urge you to find your faith in something bigger than sensory perception.

Bless you, with joy, laughter, and harmony.

On Connections

Jane Dutton, a psychologist at the **University of Michigan Business School**, gives an intriguing insight through her research. She says:

"Any point of contact with another person can potentially be a high-quality connection. One conversation, one e-mail exchange, one moment of connecting in a meeting can infuse both participants with a greater sense of vitality, giving them a bounce in their steps and a greater capacity to act."

A friend and I have begun an accountability pact (written in October 2020) to nudge each other towards crafting a daily fitness schedule. Over the past week, what I have been observing is in absolute resonance with **Jane Dutton's** findings in her psychological study. Our accountability pact is merely a simple exchange of text in the morning to remind each other of their target. That's it. As simple as that. No big words, no high-brow philosophy, no loud motivational manifestos. Just a kind nudge. I'm happy to report that, so far, it's working. Of course, I'd like to point out that we are being gentle in our approach and setting small, achievable targets first to establish habits and then building from there. We are following an idea that can be paraphrased as:

"Small steps and a big priority."

Why Connections Matter

Every once in a while, say a week, or a fortnight, my dear friend **Rohit** comes over, and we spend some time reflecting and sharing about life as it is over coffee. Just about an hour spent talking about growth, opportunities, and upliftment energised me personally tremendously. The same is the case with my friend **Rizwan**. We have our periodic audio note exchanges to talk about the glory of God, living, gratitude, and stuff like that.

I also fondly cherish visiting a dear friend's place and meeting his family a month ago. Just a brief amount of time spent laughing, sharing joy and grief was enough to keep my spirits high for a reasonable amount of time.

Our Responsibility

Investing in human capital means giving *out what you wish to receive*. This is something I swear by and has worked magically well in my life.

You give out love, respect, joy, service, admiration, support, smiles, and kindness. Do you notice something? Each of these words that I have written has a specific vibration of its own. Merely reading these words makes you feel good, doesn't it?

Make your move. Go and do your bit. It doesn't take much. One heartfelt interaction, and BOOM! We are creating a bridge rainbows between one piece of life to another. See how it keeps you afloat even in the toughest of times.

Thank you so much for reading this.

Wishing you joy, celebration, laughter, smiles and health!

Journal Prompt: Which is the most prominent human connection in your life?

Take It Easy

We are living in times where hustle and productivity are glorified. Some motivational speakers and coaches fuel the sentiments towards that idea. Hustle has its merit, of course. If you have a burning desire, you would ideally want to work with steadfast determination towards its manifestation. Productive days lead to success, no doubt.

I have started expressing doubts over the universal application of this idea, though.

Is everyone cut out for a hustle-based life?

Can everyone sustain and thrive if they just keep 'pushing' themselves?

I remember one time when our school organised a picnic (it did not sadly happen too often!), I didn't have to be woken up by my mother. I was so excited to be going for the picnic that I woke up by myself. All because I was brimming with joy and excitement.

Someone I knew had a habit of sleeping late in the morning, sometimes even until the afternoon! However, when she had to catch an early morning show of **'Avengers: End Game'**, she did not need any motivation to get up early.

What these two examples demonstrate is that there is no 'hustle' when you are full of joy and excitement about something.

The Right Goal

The **Upanishads**, an incredible source of Vedic wisdom, describe how each being in all manifestation is only after joy. We all seek it in different ways, from an ant to **Brahma** (who's credited as the creator as per the Vedic literature).

The goalpost of happiness, though, keeps shifting with each accomplishment.

Let's clear the board exams with good marks, and we'll be happy.

Once we're through intermediate school, we'll be happy.

Once we get into college, that'll be it.

Getting a well-paid job or starting a new business—that's where real happiness lies.

I wonder if we have been going about our happiness quest the wrong way.

The past couple of weeks haven't been as productive for me as I'd have ideally liked. I found myself dilly-dallying on work, my personal routine, and other things relevant to me.

Fortuitously, as I sat down to write this piece, I embraced a precious piece of wisdom—first establish yourself in joy, then do your work.

How?

- A smile

- A few minutes spent in gratitude
- Few deep breaths
- A kind word to your own self
- Affirming that I am doing the best I can and that it is okay to take it easy

BOOM! Magic. I start feeling better, and often, what does that translate into?

Productivity!

To the ones who're struggling with productivity, why don't we try and take it easy?

We may have tried harshness, criticism, and stimulants, amongst other things, let us try and normalise just being.

Dear reader, I pose you a few questions for contemplation.

How do you usually take the chill pill?

Where in your life do you need to take it easy?

Share it with me if you like.

Thank you so much for reading this.

Wish you joy, laughter, harmony, and health.

The Art Of Feedback

When I record for my podcast, I usually do it unscripted. I attribute this habit partly due to tardiness and partly to my personal preference for spontaneity. On numerous occasions, I have found that one can share more from the heart when the sharing is spontaneous.

An intelligent friend, **Niti**, who kindly and sincerely listens to my podcasts, gave beneficial feedback on the last episode. She could rightly note how I used a lot of *umms*, you know, pauses etc. She pointed out that it'll be much more useful to me if I write and follow a script. I highly appreciated the feedback because it was on the spot, well-meaning, and well-intentioned.

I could, however, note that when she gave me the feedback, there was a subconscious hesitance on her part.

Owing to perhaps an earlier experience where input wasn't taken in good stead by another person. It is entirely an assumption on my part. Maybe Niti, if and when she reads it, can concur.

This little incident got me thinking about what the proper way to correct someone is.

Each human longs for **love and acceptance**. Especially from the people around them. Therefore, it is *often telling how we also have the maximum potential to receive pain from those around us. We are taught algebra and the names and dates of historical events that may have limited significance, but not how to love ourselves and other humans.*

So often, fights and arguments do not arise from the content of the words spoken but from the tone of voice.

I'd like to share a few pointers that I have learned from my teachers on the art of giving feedback.

1. Am I the right person to give feedback?

So often, we find that older people are not just resistant to change but also take offence when a younger person tries to correct them. It doesn't matter what the intent is; maybe, some people are just not receptive to feedback from a particular individual. Brands hire celebrities to endorse their products because an ordinary person who looks up to that celeb is more likely to be influenced. These are just a couple of examples.

You do get the drift, right?

You may need to build trust and be in a position of influence before you give corrective feedback.

2. Do I have the right motive to give feedback?

Do you want to give feedback to make the other person feel small, or is your feedback coming from a genuine desire for the other person's improvement?

Is the feedback manipulative?

3. Do I know the right way to give feedback?

Saroj's husband, Manoj, wanted to surprise her after work one day. He decided to treat his wife to tomato soup when she got back home.

However, when Saroj tasted the soup, she realized the soup was bland—Manoj had forgotten to add salt. She lovingly called Manoj and fed him a spoonful. Manoj realized that he had failed to add salt. Saroj, who was tired and exhausted from work, could have criticised and ridiculed the poor husband who tried his best to please his wife. The route she took was one of smartness and empathy.

I believe humans are open to feedback. We are also sensitive creatures. If the feedback, is delivered harshly, the other person usually closes themselves up to the one giving the feedback.

4. Is it the right time?

Critical feedback given in public can most often be taken in a negative light. That same feedback if delivered in a private conversation, may yet be well received.

Sir Alex Ferguson—Manchester United's manager for twenty-six years, is one of the most extraordinary sporting personalities of all time. His managerial methods have been the subject of study at most top-level management schools in the world. I recall that Ferguson rarely criticised a player in press conferences or in public. If he did, it meant the player's career at United was over. He used to defend his players in public fiercely but, his 'hair-dryer' treatment of underperformers in private was the stuff of legends!

Suppose someone has poured out their heart and soul into something, and another one comes and blatantly criticises it, deserving or not. In that case, it can cause a massive blow to their morale.

Words have tremendous power.

An Episode From The Life Of The Smiling Panda

One day I posted a tweet in response to another's question about **Buddha and Krishna**. Someone I used to consider a dear friend pulled out a previous blog post of mine and replied to that tweet with the intent to pull me down.

I had been observing for some time that the person only engaged with me in the online world when she found something to pick on or to be sarcastic about.. My immediate reaction was anger. I hadn't even been sending her my blog posts. Neither had she ever interacted with one!

Fortunately, rather than punching out my rage on the keyboard of my phone, I decided to choose a measured response. I asked her to talk to me only when she was willing to display appropriate behaviour.

Well, she hasn't spoken to me since.

Good riddance, I suppose!

I was a bit disturbed the evening this incident happened. I got on a call with one of my best friends, **Sheetal**, and she wondered if we were too sensitive about things?

I opined that it'd be better to be sensitive and not cause a chain reaction of negativity than to lap shit up and one day explode.

Sheetal's query was answered just the next day by the

Universe, which keeps tabs on our inner workings.

The next day, I posted an update shared by a college classmate in our college group for a bit of frolic. Within a few minutes of posting it, one friend texted me on personal chat and asked me to delete that post. He went something like:

"Hey, please remove that post. The others can get quite crazy with their comments sometimes... listen, I love and respect you, and because I am a well-wisher, that is why I have made this demand. If you think I am wrong, please forgive me."

I was stunned and humbled by the contrast between two people and their respective approaches to wanting to correct me. One chose sarcasm and ended up making me feel bad, while the other corrected me in a way that'll stay with me for life!

And via the above two incidents, the Universe itself demonstrated what technique works and what doesn't.

Also, who gets to decide what is bearable and what is not?

How can there be a universal norm of what kind of 'jokes' are okay and why one shouldn't be touchy-feely about them?

2020 marked a pivotal moment in my life journey where I started establishing boundaries.

'Do unto yourself as you do to others.'

I feel incredibly fortunate that I have understood the

immense power of words. It is an ever-growing practice to either saying things that are truthful, sweet, and cause upliftment or not speak at all. I feel it isn't wrong to expect the same.

Thank you for reading until the end. I hope I was able to add something new and useful to your life. God bless you with lots of sweetness and goodness.

Journal Prompt: Which is the best or most useful feedback you have ever received?

Circle Of Goodness

My dear friend Aditi shared an inspiring story of an acquaintance of hers who recovered from depression by reading books and talking with her.

Aditi was incredibly kind to share the news and somehow even share the credit with me. She told me that she had shared books with her acquaintance that had been recommended to her by me at one point.

In my podcast episode What Goes Around Comes Around, I spoke about the unwanted *karmic frisbee*.

One person who dumps their anger on another starts this kind of cycle.

Let's say, person A gets angry at person B and uses harsh words. Person B, if capable of retorting, would do so, if not, they'd suppress the hurt. If person B is not on the path of spirit and healing, he/she would then dump the anger on someone who is in a position of subordination to B, say C. C continues with the cycle. If, along the cycle, people find no human to take out their frustration and anger, they would do so upon animals or inanimate objects even.

I recently read a quote online that I found to be profound and impactful. It went something like:

"If you never heal from what hurts you, you'll bleed on people who did not cut you."

It becomes so significant in such a context to be part of the right circle and not a vicious negative one.

We can all now gauge from the above example why it is said that **hurt people, hurt people**. In the same breath, I'd like to add that the lesson from the story of Aditi's acquaintance coming out of depression with her help and presence is that:

Healed people, heal people.

After listening to Aditi and the story she shared, I started thinking about how I read the two books I go on recommending to anyone willing to be on the path of growth.

My father brought the **Gita** in 1998 at the insistence of a devotee in **Iskcon**. He kept the book in our home library and as is the case with many of us—we may worship the book but do not read it—so was the case with Gita.

Bhagavan Krishna inspired me to pick it up in 2007.

That transformed my life into an unrecognisable state. It has helped me serve almost everyone who has come into my life. Notice the incredible synchronicity and positive circle created by one right decision made by my father.

A decade later, I had one of the worst phases of my life. I had a significant fallout with someone I considered an idol, left theatre, broke up with the first love of my life, and excused myself from Civil engineering for good. Jobless, aimless, full of self-doubts, guilt-tripping myself for all the challenges life threw my way, and disconnected with even **Krishna**. I, fortunately, sought therapy, which, in a way, has led to a better state of life where I am right now. However, another important event occurred that led to Aditi's acquaintance's healing in one way. Life is so mystical, I tell you!

Back then, in September 2017, My friend **Sheetal** sent me a book that had the most profound impact on me since reading the **Bhagavad Gita** as a teenager in 2007. Here's the fascinating part: The lessons I derived from the book helped me, and they helped Sheetal herself a year later when she found herself challenged by life.

Karmic frisbee at its best!

When I was down in the dumps, Sheetal called and said I'm sending you this fantastic book called, '<u>You Can Heal Your Life</u>' by **Louise Hay**. She told me a friend of hers had been applying teachings from the book experiencing profound changes. I should try it out as well. As mentioned, I ascribe the book to be the second most impactful book in my life.

I'm fascinated by how one act of heartfelt sharing by one individual can be for so incredibly impactful and positive ripple effect for so many lives.

Aditi's sharing helped me reaffirm the power of sharing positive things in the world. It also inspires me further to be a part of a positive life cycle than a cycle of any lower vibrational energy.

I humbly invite you as well to join the circle of positivity. Unabashedly share the good in your life and serve. Let's heal, bond, grow, and transform together.

Thank you for reading this.

Journal Prompt: Think about an act of kindness performed by you towards another or you being at the receiving end that created a ripple of goodness around.

Life Is Just Not Easy

"O Master of the Universe, I pray that we keep getting more and more miseries because in miserable times we have had your darshan (presence), and one who gets your darshan doesn't have to return to the whirlpool of birth and death."

SRIMADA BHAGAVATAM 1.8.25

When Bhagavan **Shri Krishna** is leaving for His kingdom **Dwarka,** having instated **Yudhisthira** as the rightful ruler of the world after the **Mahabhharata War**, **Queen Kunti** comes in front of His chariot and offers prayers. The quote above is one verse from the soulful prayers offered by her to Shri Krishna in the first canto of the eighth chapter of the **Bhagavatam**. This prayer is one of the most celebrated prayers of Bhagavatam and one that is dear to devotees of Shri

Krishna. As you can see, the specialty here is that it's strange to find someone asking the divine for more miseries in life. Usually, prayers involve people asking the divine for "daily bread," wealth, health, riches, love (from other humans) etc. Who asks for pain?

A Whirlpool of Repeated Miseries

Within the last month, a friend's mother had to be hospitalised thanks to the virus; another friend's father passed away due to cancer. A few days ago, another friend's husband tested positive for the Wuhan virus, and someone's cancer has started to spread. All while we continue to come to terms with—the anxiety about the virus, the economic pushback, and the emotional challenges of coping with the 'new normal'.

Yep, life is just not easy.

Whether you pray for miseries like **Queen Kunti** or you don't, suffering is something that is definitely going to arrive in life. At least there is one bit of certainty in an otherwise uncertain world!

Queen Kunti's Formula

In the **Mahabharata**, the **Pandavas**, despite being the most extraordinary people, suffered calamitous situations throughout their lives. **Kunti** herself was widowed at a young age, suffered all life reversals along with her children, and subsequently saw all her son, **Karna,** and grandchildren killed in the great war.

Her response, though?

She's asking **Krishna** for more miseries because somehow she has the cognisance that she is something more significant than the circumstances in her life. And besides, she has found both solace and the ultimate solution in surrendering to the Supersoul, i.e., **Krishna**.

Someone may ask, but, Kushagra, I'm not religious. I cannot submit to some Supersoul or God.

Fair enough. I agree that not everyone is blessed with the *vision of Queen Kunti.*

"Bahūnām janmanām ante jñānavān mām prapadyate"

BHAGAVAD GITA, 7.19

After many many births, one who is enlightened by actual knowledge surrenders to the Supersoul.

What about the commoners like us who do not have either the tolerance of **Queen Kunti** or her wisdom to devote ourselves to the Supreme?

If You Get Nervous, Focus On Service

Once, when I was doing an oracle card reading for a friend who was anxious about the state of his life, I got a beautiful card.

The message on the card read:

"If you get nervous, focus on service."

As I sat down to write this blog, the angels reminded me of this card once again. Life has been a bit overwhelming over the past few months. While we are powerless over external circumstances, we can always strive to ease others's lives. We can spread a little smile, a spark of joy to someone else. Not because of some 'Karma theory' or moral principles, but because the act of service itself makes one feel alive and happy in the now.

Wouldn't that be the best gift?

As I reflect upon Shri Krishna's life, I find that throughout His life, He dedicated His divine presence for the betterment of others.

- He left His beloved **Vrindavan** to free the residents of **Mathura** from the tyranny of **Kams**.

- Made **Ugrasena** the king of **Dwarka** even though Krishna Himself was the most qualified person.

- Helped King **Yuddhisthira** conduct a '**Rajsuya Yajña**' that established the king's supremacy.

- Became a messenger of peace and tried to evade the great war.

- Became **Arjuna's charioteer** in the great war.

- Saved **Bhima** from certain death at the hands of **Dhritarashtra**.

- Got cursed by **Gandhari** on behalf of the Pandavas, as naturally the curse would've been directed towards them.

Perhaps that is the secret sauce to going through existence. Krishna refers to it as 'दुखलायम्' (place of misery) in the **Bhagavad Gita**—*Keep a smile and offer some service to life around.*

An Attitude Shift

If the above doesn't resonate with you, then we may focus on cultivating a resilient attitude through the inspirational example set by great people like **Kunti**.

Our epics are full of stories of triumph after prolonged suffering. Be it the **Mahabharata** or the **Ramayana**. One reason why these stories are taught and propagated is to inspire us towards the realization that no matter what kind of adversity comes into our lives, we can overcome it.

Acceptance of the present moment is that a magical gift that anyone can use to transform any suffering.

I love how **Sadhguru** puts it. He says if you look back at the happiest moments of your life, one common thread in each is that you were all-embracing of those moments. There was a complete *acceptance* of what was happening. No resistance.

Reversals in life will come no matter what you do or who you are. You can have billions in wealth, millions of followers, look like a supermodel, be on top of your career, and have thriving relationships, but problems will still find a way to creep up.

The question is: what makes life easier despite the challenges?

Moaning, complaining, and embitterment.

OR

Graceful acceptance of the situation and then working towards overcoming it?

If you're going through a hard time in your life right now, I send you blessings and positive vibes. May the divine bless you with inner strength and wisdom. May you cultivate an attitude that overcomes each challenge.

Journal Prompt: When you think about existence, what is your perspective on life?

Honest Confessions Of An Angry man

I found it funny that recently two people, an old friend and a well-meaning acquaintance, reached out to me to ask if I had written something about anger.

You may ask, 'What's funny in the above scenario, Kushagra?'

Well, it is funny to me because it's like someone asking Hitler if he's written something on non-violence or asking an ultra left or ultra right leaning person about logic.

I have been working with anger issue since a while now. I even took professional help from Miss Priyanka Bhargava (a clinical hypnotherapist) and her profound psychological shadow work methods. So, it wouldn't be wrong to at least attempt to share my story.

Previously, I'd written something on anger in <u>Gates of Heaven and Hell</u> (read it for a fantastic **Zen** story and some wisdom from Shri **Krishna** on the topic) (we can mention the chapter number and page number here). As I went through the piece, I realized I had presented a lot of philosophy but not my realizations. As I move ahead in my life journey, I find personal realizations and experiences >>> philosophy.

Anger Story

Memories of Anger stem from my teens. I was bullied at home often and sometimes even at school as a kid. As I started growing, I couldn't tolerate even a tiny caustic remark against me; neither could I accept what I perceived as injustice. While I couldn't give it back at home, outside situations started being convenient. By my teens, I'd even lost the fear of being beaten up (I wasn't a strong kid inside or out), and I started realising the tongue is mightier than the sword! The tongue could cause more lasting damage than a physical injury ever could. I used this knowledge to my advantage as much as possible.

There used to be an inexplicable delight in 'giving it back' to someone who caused trouble. Anger gave such a maddening high of power that the loss of sanity that came with it seemed like a small price to pay. Most importantly, all the years of suppression could find an outlet in anger.

No one can ever again suppress me!

I refuse to be treated like crap!

If you are bad, I am your dad! (A Facebook page inspired this one!)

Such 'high-end' thoughts became the fulcrum of my thought process and life. Anger used to possess me so intensely that I now recall that on many occasions, my body would literally be shaking. My vocal cords developed wonderfully well thanks to all the shouting that came attached with the *gift of anger.*

Looking back, I find it miraculous how I survived not getting bashed up on so many occasions.

I remember there was a short period in 2007 when **Shri Krishna** found me when all these human issues ceased to matter. Only Him, and His teachings mattered. Anger became a thing of the past. I remember when I joined the school after immersions in the **Gita and the Bhagavatam**, a classmate threw a paper ball towards me. The former me would not just have thrown the paper ball back at her face but would've followed it up with a volley of other paper balls. And perhaps even throwing water or whatever else I could lay hands on. But, on that occasion, I picked the paper ball and returned it to her gently with a smile.

I remember my dear friend **Sarvesh,** who observed the entire scene, came up to me immediately and checked if I was in a 'mentally healthy/stable state'. He said and I quote,

"Teri tabiyat toh theek hai...? Fever toh nahi hai."

Well, I was feverish with the intoxication of **Krishna**. It is a shame, though, that this change was not permanent. I went back to my usual ways quite soon, and this time I added spiritual ego and bigotry to it as well.

I remember a spiritual counsellor who met me once asking me to check my anger. She narrated to me the story of **Shri Krishna** and **Shishupal**—how Krishna used to forgive Shishupal's hundred offences each day. But, I had made up my mind. We only engage in 'idol' worship, ma'am. We don't follow the path shown by **Krishna**. Nor do we choose to learn from the way He conducted His life. Nope.

Who cares if **Krishna** or **Rama** did not get needlessly angry—they're divine. Mortals like me who 'worship' deities only engage in judging others. Who drinks, who's eating animals, who is doing drugs—that's what we concern ourselves with and get an unabashed high by comparing my 'piety' with their 'fallen' state. Out of the eighteen chapters of the **Gita**, one hundred and twenty-one chapters of the **Bhagavatam** dedicated to Shri **Krishna**, this is what I apparently learned.

When a lady in my life showed me in the mirror by saying, "What's the point of all this if you can't behave nicely, I went full *Rowdies*!" (*TU... TU BATAYEGI MUJHE... yaar* Ranvijay, I'm done.)

Combining the power of anger with harsh words, I caused a lot of emotional damage to others. I shamelessly admit that it felt (still does) SOOOO good to inflict the damage.

What did it cost, though?

- Shattered Relationships. Often beyond repair.
- My peace of mind.
- Precious energy, which I could have used more productively.

- Guilt.
- Shame.
- Regret.

Is it even worth going through so much anger?

Anger can have constructive uses. I'm sure **Sri Hanuman jee** would have been angry when he burned **Lanka** (Ravan's ego) down.

Arjuna had to be angry to shoot millions of arrows at the Kaurava army in the War of the Mahabharata.

How does it help me, though?

As far as I see, almost every unconscious expression of anger has cost me dearly.

Why Does Anger Come Up?

In one of my recent therapy sessions with Miss Priyanka, we focused on anger, as I mentioned above. Without getting into the exact details, I'll share with you what she deduced from my situation.

"You don't define your boundaries. When someone tramples upon them, anger has become the only resort."

"Anger can be replaced by assertiveness. Being assertive about what is significant to you is not unreasonable. Choose assertiveness when you can."

Adding to the above nuggets of wisdom, I'd add that anger has also often arisen when I've had preconceived notions about people and how they should behave.

"How can my girlfriend act contrary to how I imagined her to be?"

"How can my friend not notice all the good vibes I share and not reciprocate even a tiny bit?"

"How can that driver cut me off?"

"Why won't anybody mind queues in this country?"

"Why can't China eat sensibly?"

In all of the above circumstances, you notice how anger stems from **control issues**. In a brazen display of profound stupidity, I'm trying to control something that is usually beyond me.

Sadhguru emphasises the incredible concept of responsibility: while you can respond to everything, your action remains limited. Response stems from consciousness, while reactive states of anger stem from an unorganised mindset.

In the above scenarios, I cannot control how my friend, girlfriend, fellow driver on the road, or people in public places behave. I can, at best, take care of my 'response-ability' in any given situation.

Is There A Way Out?

Yes, there is.

It can take time and patience. May even take a lifetime. However, it is worth it.

I've been trying to embrace this angry child within me who is still upset with the mean world that feels it's okay to be rude and pull others down without rhyme or reason. I use the word embraced carefully because you cannot fight something as powerful as anger. You cannot wake up in the morning and say, 'Hey, today, I'm not going to get angry.' The chances are high that you would.

Last week, when I was sitting in meditation, I felt an immense surge of anger and hate boiling up within me. The experience of it left me anxious for a while. How can this experience surface when I'm supposed to be engaged in a spiritual practise?

Wisdom entails that a proper spiritual process is about pulling forth your darkest sides from within for you to witness and transform.

Upon reflection, I realize the anger surfaced because I have been trying to move away from the destructive use of this energy. But, the energy is very much a part of me. I can't disown it altogether.

Are there any practical steps one can take to manage anger?

Yes. Practical steps, for sure. Not just spiritual and philosophical woo-woo. Below, let me enunciate a few ideas.

1. Running

Run when you're angry. Literally if it is possible. It is better to burn some calories than to burn a relationship down. Some people also advise leaving the place where the anger arose. Go to another room. In ancient times, there used to be कोप भवन, i.e. a particular space to vent out. They recognised that it isn't safe to let out the potent energy of anger just about anywhere.

2. Punch a pillow/Boxing bag

Again. We are recognising and giving a place for to our anger to find expression. Think of **Captain America** in the **Avengers** movie. Punch, punch, punch away the energy that is rising within you. If not a punching bag, then a pillow. As **Osho** said, the pillow is a **Buddha**. It doesn't react to you. Bare your emotions there.

3. Shout/vent out

If it is possible—test out your vocal cords and shake off that rising energy within you. However, you need to ensure you're not in public vicinity lest you scare someone. Not being in the vicinity of a human in a country like India is extremely hard. So we move on to the next option.

4. Record an audio note

Express yourself. Why are you angry? Curse, criticise,

vent, and read out the charges. Say whatever you would say to the person (in case it is a person you're angry with) in the audio. Just don't send that audio to anyone. Listen to it after recording. Would you be proud of expressing this a few days or, say, even a few hours down the line? You will not only expend some energy but also gain perspective as to what may be the wise choice of words in expressing yourself with assertiveness and not angry outbursts.

5. Hypno-drama

This is a technical term we use in hypnotherapy. The purpose of Hypno-drama is to create imaginary scenarios in our heads, wherein we are safely able to process and express our anger towards someone or something. This can be hugely beneficial in expurgating traumatic experiences from the mind and heart. I've found it extremely useful on a personal level to play out specific jarring experiences while reprogramming my mind with life-supporting thoughts. The time I used to be active in offering clinical hypnotherapy sessions, I knew many clients who felt the same benefits. A word of advise or caution: One must delve into such kind of process under the guidance of an able therapist.

6. Journaling

A fantastic technique that I picked up from a book I read this year is to write a letter expressing anguish to someone who's affronted us. We don't need to send that letter. Just write your heart out. Now, this is basic, and you may have even heard of this technique that writing/journaling helps you process your feelings better. However, the catch is to imagine now the kind of response you would ideally like to receive and write that down as if the person who offended you were writing a letter of apology. Once again, there is no involvement of another—you retain the power in your world. Quite magnificent and safe.

7. Action and Reaction

The laws of the universe are absolute. It's a no brainer that what we give out comes back. And hence, one has to ask themselves what kind of energy am I willing to put out there in the universe?

Would I be comfortable receiving it back for when it arrives?

If you are okay with the consequences, feel free to choose your reactions the way you like. As for me, I'm now seriously reviewing the pros and cons of spending this precious and intense energy of anger randomly. I additionally am feeling the pain of what my unconscious reactions have cost me.

If you have any suggestions on the topic, please do enlighten me.

A complimentary listen to this piece is an episode from my podcast: What Goes Around Comes Around. You may wish to check that out as well.

God bless you.

Journal Prompt: Reflect upon a time when an

(unhealthy) expression of anger cost you dear.

Be Like Jack

One of my favourite tv shows is <u>This Is Us</u>. Available on **Hotstar** and **Amazon Prime** (at least was when I was writing this piece) this emotional drama has some incredible writing and performances.

In one episode, one of the main characters of the show, *Rebecca*, gets involved in an accident because she was talking on the phone and not paying attention to the road. As she is getting admitted to the hospital, she keeps fretting about how her husband and kids would react.

When the husband, *Jack*, reaches the hospital, *Rebecca* starts putting up a defence for her present condition by uttering something like:

"Oh, I'm so sorry...this happened, then that happened and the next thing I knew..."

Jack cuts her off by saying,

"Hey, it's okay. It's happened now. Just tell me how you are right now?"

These lines impacted me so tremendously that I'm making an entire piece inspired out of it!

Everyone one screws up. Me, you, big people, small people, the wise and otherwise...just like sadness is part of the human deal, so are mistakes, I believe.

It's not as much about the mistakes though, it's how we end up reacting to the mistakes.

Personally, I have experienced lots of angst at others' and my own mistakes in life. The angst gets repeated again and again as I review the problem, keep harping on what could've been, why it happened and instead of moving on, I end up staying stuck.

When *Jack* said to his wife, "It's okay, it's now happened", it jolted me to realize the power of acceptance.

Jack isn't doing something phenomenal here. He isn't propounding some profound philosophy; he isn't quoting the scriptures. All *Jack* does is accept.

Boom!

Yet, this simple little act of acceptance can be so tricky.

I find myself wondering, how'd it be more like *Jack* and say, it's okay, it has happened. Let's move on. Let's see what can be done now. There is no erasing the past. There is no time machine available (yet) to go behind and change something.

One of the pillars of self-love is acceptance of the self—the good, the bad, the ugly, the evil.

A few months ago, I made a huge boo boo. It cost me a considerable sum of money. I was quite shattered, honestly. **Shri Krishna**'s words from the **Bhagavad Gita** helped about accepting life's reversals with grace. Support from some friends like *Sheetal* and *Rizwan* (in whom I confided) is always a blessing.

However, what one of my mentors and teacher, Miss Priyanka told me blew me away completely.

"Kush, the question here is can you accept this not so smart, supposedly stupid self of yours as well? Can you love this part of yourself too?"

Self-love isn't just about growth and improvement. It's also about acceptance of our errors.

While we're working at accepting ourselves more, we would find it easier to accept others' follies as well. Coming from personal experience, I've witnessed that our external behaviour is always a mirror of our internal conditioning.

A person with solid self-esteem wouldn't put others down.

A person who can accept his or her own self would quickly adapt to others.

One who can forgive themselves can also forgive others easily.

What a complicated, beautiful, painful, fascinating experience it is to be human, folks!

Thank you so much for reading this.

I wish you laughter, joy, harmony and peace.

Journal Prompt: What aspect of your life needs more acceptance right now?

Wish You A Happy Ending

The show Modern Love is very well made and sweetness inducing. It is available on **Amazon Prime** and I highly recommend it.

The show comprises of about 30 minute long episodes of eight different stories about people living in *New York*. Modern love, the prime tv show has been dramatized from *NYT's column* by the same name. The final episode gives the viewers a glimpse of what's up in the lives of the people we saw in previous episodes.

Watching the final episode of season one, I started wondering about all the people that I've met in my life and the ones who no longer configure in my story. What remains is just memories. I found myself strangely nostalgic and ruminative.

Each human being has such a unique story. When we

see such stories being represented on the visual medium, we get hooked. The basis of these stories is, of course, human life.

In each person's life and story, they are the protagonist. Each and every person they encounter is just supporting cast.

I wonder that does anybody think of how a particular character's life story must be shaping up? Or are we too occupied to delve into such trivial matters?

I often ruminate over what must have become of a character I encounter in a book or a show or movie.

Did they really get a happily ever after?

Did they manage to reconcile with that loss?

Did they have another adventure in life as the one that was shared by the storyteller with us?

I extend this chain of thought to the people whom I've lost to life, i.e., the ones whose life has led them to a new journey wherein, my part is over. Their memories however remain.

It is quite fascinating to think someone who occupied so much mental (and in some ways physical) space in the play of your life may now be completely anonymous.

Think of that ex or that childhood friend you've lost touch with.

Perhaps that Uber driver with whom you had a genuinely good conversation.

That fellow you met and got acquainted with in the train journey?

The one you promised to keep in touch, but you didn't?

As I write this, I am reminded of a Sikh couple I encountered on my train journeys to Uttar Pradesh as a kid. Imagine meeting the same people in the same train coach on different train journeys! When I recognized the kind lady, she smiled and said, "the world is a small place."

Is it really?

Or is it not?

Isn't it fascinating to think that no one's story gets affected even when someone walks away?

There may always be a void, but we move on. **Irrfan Khan** left his body, but roles will still be written.

Characters he could've portrayed would be portrayed by other people. We may not even notice the absence much after a while. We can only rejoice the memories.

And so when someone walks out your life, or you do, do remember that the show goes on. The roles get assigned to different people and what is meant for us to experience comes one way or the other.

I recall **Dr Wayne Dyer**'s words:

"Consider being like a mirror, and reflect what comes into your life without judgement or opinions. Be unattached to all who come into your life by not demanding that they stay, go, or appear, at your whim."

Christopher Nolan wrote a letter to all the Batman fans after he'd completed the epic **Dark Knight Trilogy**. In that letter, one particular line caught my attention:

"I will miss Batman. But I don't think he will miss me. He isn't particularly sentimental!"

Maybe the people whom I've lost to life may no longer miss me or think of my journey as I think about theirs. Perhaps they are like Batman—not particularly sentimental.

No matter what happens to anyone's story once I've taken an exit, and whether or not they think of me, all I wish is that they have a happy ending.

Don't you?

Do a recall of all the people who showed up as characters in the play of life. It's all been perfect.

That ex who left you was meant to teach you, self-love.

The disciplinarian parent meant to instil order.

The people who stayed are also part of the perfect law of life.

Here's a thought (affirmation) for you to ruminate over and connected to our theme today:

Everyone I need for my life journey will show up, and they'll be perfect in every way for whatever need you to have at that time.

Journal Prompt: Who from your life journey and story do you wish a happy ending?

Personal Power Leakage

"I was talking politely; however, the other one was rude, so I decided to mirror the other."

It has often happened to me that I am in a good mood, projecting cheer and good vibes to the people I am interacting with. However, if an individual fails to reciprocate the same kind of vibes, I lose my element.

Today (the day I am writing this blog), I felt giddy.

I was enthusiastic, energetic, and a bit like **Preity Zinta** when she realized she was in love with **SRK** in the movie **Kal Ho Na Ho**.

I think using smileys while communicating virtually with people is like keeping a smile when we talk to people in the real world. One appears more courteous to the other person.

Today was a lots of smileys kind of day.

Speaking cheerfully to a friend over *WhatsApp*, I felt that their response was a bit cold. My ship of giddiness started sinking in the waters of another person's perceived cold attitude.

Fortunately, **Shri Krishna** (the universe or divine) within the heart reminded me that how the other person behaves or talks to me need not affect my mood or cheer.

Misplaced Expectations

Often in the past, I have found myself despondent over the expectation (darn you, expectations) that people will mirror my cheer and enthusiasm. Also, at other times I expect (darn you, again) that others should not reflect my weariness, anger, ego and other lower vibrational states.

So totally unfair on other people!

Take the friend's case whom I was speaking to in the morning. Perhaps the friend had just:

- Woken up and cranky
- Had an argument with a loved one at home
- Been served with *tinde kee sabzi* for breakfast
- Felt constipated
- Accidentally saw an atrocious reel on Instagram

Who knows?

And I did not ask.

Even if nothing untoward was up in their lives, perhaps they just weren't feeling as up to the conversation and the day as I was. After all, we all have our personal waxing and waning phases, like the Moon.

Let no self-help guru, coach, or influencer fool you into thinking that everyone has it together every day.

No, sir/ma'am.

There is always something up the sleeve of the universe to remind you: everything is impermanent.

Allowing your mood to be dictated by another's response is so comically imbecile!

I now laugh at my younger self for all the times I took life, myself, and others too seriously.

Victor E Frankl, a Holocaust survivor, says in his pathbreaking book called **Man's Search For Meaning,** (paraphrasing),

"All kinds of freedom can be taken away from you but your freedom of attitude towards a situation."

Precious words of wisdom from someone who managed to keep himself sane during an extremely challenging life situation; learned from it and helped so many people once he was free.

Sadhguru says that it's a form of slavery to be dependent on another person for your happiness. It is like, as he says, you've given the remote control of your life to another person. They can press a specific button, and that can elicit a particular response from you. There is no right way to exist for sure.

I'm so happy I chose not to feel bothered by the friend's lack of my 'perceived' cheer when I spoke to them in the morning. I made a decision that I'm gonna make the most of the happy vibe given by **Shri Krishna** (universe) today and spread that.

Such healthy behaviour has not been a constant in my life, frankly. I owe a lot of it to developing my inner power and strengthening my best parts through specific practises and tools.

Want to know more about tools to increase personal power?

Flip to the next chapter.

Until then, thank you so much for staying with me until the end of this piece.

Joy, harmony, and peace.

Journal Prompt: How do you usually find yourself giving your power away?

Four Tips To Cultivate Inner Power And Freedom

1. **Say No**

A few months earlier, I burst out on a dear friend for something that did not merit bursting out. Even though I apologised to the friend later, when I got over from the negative intoxication of anger and ego, I tried to dig deeper into the issue.

I realized that sometimes you fail to set boundaries for even the most intimate of relationships. The other person, unaware of what you're thinking within, may unknowingly trample upon the unsaid, invisible boundary.

Often in life, you agree to meet, talk, engage, or do anything else that you don't want to do only because you do not want to risk offending a dear one in your life.

What happens then?

All the suppression comes out in the form of unwanted emotional outbursts.

My outburst at the friend was not the result of a single conversation or issue. It was instead the buildup of all the times I gave in half-heartedly to engagements with him when I did not want to.

Saying no sounds simple in theory, but in practise, it can be hard. I have, for sure, found it hard!

The social conditioning is such that whenever I say no, I feel a sense of discomfort and guilt—saying no to a call, a meeting, or even an invitation.

Saying no to that late-night conversation over WhatsApp because you love your schedule and sleep more is not easy, trust me. But if you can cultivate the habit of saying no when your heart feels like it, you develop a lot of inner power.

Kelly Morrigan, in her lovely book, **'Tell Me More'** sums up her thoughts on saying no really well.

I wrap up this section with a few of her quotes from the book:

"Learn to say no. And when you do, don't complain and don't explain. Every excuse you make is like an invitation to ask you again in a different way."

"Little noes prepare us for the big noes that define the major movements of our lives. The job we shouldn't take, the relationship we must leave, the deal that seems shady. No, finally, to another drink, no to abuse, no to getting back together. No to extreme life-saving measures."

"There's hardly a positive intention associated with no. Except self-preservation."

2. Be Upfront With Your Expectations

There is a useful lesson from my first relationship that I still draw upon when I find my ego inflated. Upon witnessing my angry outbursts, my then-girlfriend used to remark,

"What is the use of all this spirituality if you do not know how to behave?"

The words stung back then, but almost six years (and counting) later, I see and realize the relevance of her words.

Wise ones say that the power of yoga, prayers, meditations, etc. is manifested not on the prayer mat but in day to day activities.

The reason the anger was manifested towards her was due to unfulfilled expectations.

Some say that setting expectations for people is like chucking a stone in the air and complaining later when it falls upon your head.

I humbly differ.

Setting expectations isn't the problem.

The problem is assuming the other person is a mind reader.

As human beings, I find that it is nearly impossible to be unconditional in our dealings.

I do not berate myself or anyone else for setting expectations as long as the communication of those expectations is healthy and respectful. You express and define your expectations clearly, and then you do not feel entitled to their fulfilment.

I love my realization that having expectations is good, but entitlement, not.

Once you can be authentic about your feelings and desires, you experience a greater sense of power and freedom.

3. Speak Your Truth

This one is essentially an extension of the second principle and links to principle number one as well.

Have you ever noticed that when you are trying to say no to something, you can use a lie to extricate yourself from the situation?

Your colleague or friend asks, "Up for dinner tonight?"

You want to rest or have something else planned. However, not wanting to 'offend' the friend, you retort with a lie, "Oh, actually, this person in my family is not well."

"Oh, I have a headache."

Yep, the headache excuse is not just used by men and women to avoid sex.

Have you also noticed how you feel a sense of discomfort in your heart when you lie?

I sure have.

That discomfort comes from the spirit, which loves authenticity and transparency.

It is a great irony that even a person who is a habitual liar gets offended upon confronting a lie. The power of truth is such that even crooked people internally respect the truthful one.

But does authenticity only entail truthful words?

Not always.

Authenticity lies in expressing your truth with gentleness. The truth cannot and should not be a bitter pill. It should lead to freedom and peace. One's expression of truth must not injure or harm another on an emotional or mental level. It is one thing that I have personally observed that needs tremendous work.

Vedic books say that authenticity in speech is austerity in itself—which in turn leads the person to immense power in speech and manifestation via the power of words.

A person who is transparent in speech and conduct has nothing to fear—That gives them tremendous personal power.

4. Be True To Your Word

When you make tall claims to yourself and others and fail to follow them through, that causes a lot of personal power to wane away.

Say you resolved to be regular with an activity at the beginning of the year. However, in your enthusiasm, you failed to dovetail the resolution with a logical and achievable plan. The resolution fails, and you feel miserable.

Always start with small commitments and begin with yourself.

Say you set the alarm clock for 6 a.m. the next morning. If you manage to wake up and get going with your day, you feel a sense of tremendous self-satisfaction within yourself. Such a 'seemingly small' achievement can fuel you and enhance the quality of your other engagements.

Observe the areas of your life that need improvement. Start making incremental changes by setting small and achievable targets.

Do that one, Surya Namaskar.

Meditate for two minutes.

Write that one line in the journal.

Eat one healthy meal a day.

Read one page a day.

Just commit and follow through.

It is not easy to tame the mind; however, with a gentle

yet firm approach, it eases up.

I sincerely hope the four ideas that I have shared with you resonate and add value to your life. The execution of these ideas may not be easy and smooth; expect the ego to create obstacles. Such obstacles, though, can be overcome.

On that note, I wish to leave you with an inspirational quote from the **Bhagavad Gita by Bhagavan Shri Krishna:**

"That which in the beginning maybe just like poison but at the end is just like nectar and which awakens one to self-realization is said to be happiness in the mode of goodness."

BHAGAVAD GITA, 18.37

Wishing you the power to uplift yourself and those around you.

Journal Prompt: Make a list of ways to plug your personal power leakage.

I Won't Kill You But I Don't Have To Save You Either

Young Bruce witnesses his parents murder right before his eyes. That one incident leads him on a journey that gives us the legend of Batman.

The story of **Batman,** created by **Bob Kane,** has inspired numerous people since its inception. No interpretation, however, has been as magical and engaging as the one by **Mr Nolan.** Not on a cinematic medium anyway.

The **Dark Knight Trilogy** is a masterpiece in every aspect. Acting, writing, direction, visuals, and music. You name it.

In the first part of the trilogy, **Batman Begins**, Bruce avows not to kill.. He may beat criminals up to a pulp, hang them from the top of buildings, and drive dangerously on the streets of Gotham (sometimes on rooftops even), but no killing.

In the climax scene of Batman Begins, Batman is on a tube train that's about to crash into a building. His nemesis and teacher, *Ra's Al Ghul,* is engaged in a battle with him. This Ra's guy is a deranged loony who thinks the world needs a reset button (oh wait, that actually makes a lot of sense).

Ghul has unleashed a vaporised chemical upon Gotham. That chemical, once inhaled through the lungs, gives human beings free goosebumps. Of course Batma spoils this ~~noble~~ evil plan of Ra's.

When Batman manages to pin down Ra's, he has two options:

1. Either fly away solo

2. Take Ra's with him and save him.

He chooses the first option.

Before flying away, Batman says to Ra's

"I don't have to kill you, but I don't have to save you either."

Okay To Fly Away?

People can end up draining you.

Relationships, work, or family—the things that are significant parts of life—can sometimes become a pain.

The very things that once gave you joy can turn into horrors.

What should I do in such a scenario?

Can you 'kill' something (a relationship) that is precious to you?

Can you be an aggressor towards something that's nourished you in the past?

Not really. It's never easy.

In fact, the premise of one of the most incredible scriptures known to humans, the **Bhagwad Gita,** is the same. *Arjuna* gets cold feet at the prospect of engaging in warfare against his filial connections.

Fortunately, not everyone has to go through such dramatic circumstances.

Do you speak up against a perceived injustice within the family?

Do you let a loved one know that their behaviour is off track?

Is it okay to walk away from something that doesn't bring joy to your heart and soul?

If we were to take into account, the wisdom of Batman in Batman Begins, most certainly YES!

Give It Back?

Expressions of grief and *explanations* of anger can be freeing. The problem is that one doesn't know when it can get out of hand.

It's still okay to try. Try to make people see reason and sense.

What if they're not willing to relent?

Sensitive people face a lot of moral issues. They are slighted by a hint of harsh behaviour from others. But if they give it back, they end up wallowing in guilt.

It's best to take the middle path.

It's okay to walk away.

Walking away doesn't mean you've closed the door; it means you are willing to choose your peace over another's drama.

Aeroplane Wisdom

The flight attendants carefully instruct and demonstrate to the passengers that in a case of emergency, it's advised to first attend to yourself then thinking of helping another. The catch is that, *if you cannot breathe yourself properly, how can you expect to serve another?*

It's alright to put on that oxygen mask.

It's alright to choose yourself.

A societal construct of morality should not let you wilt in an equation that robs you of your soul's light.

If someone else cannot see your light and if another is unwilling to mend their ways, hey, it's okay to fly away.

I conclude by sharing a quote from Bhagwan Shri Krishna, Bhagwad Gita, 2.66

"And how can there be any happiness without peace?"

Love, laughter, harmony, and peace

Journal Prompt: What kind of behaviour would make you walk away from a relationship?

We All Deserve A Jambvan

One may hardly find a person born in the land of *Bharat* who is not aware of the story of the **Ramayana**.

In the **Sundarkand** section of the Ramayana that primarily expounds the glories of **Shri Hanuman**, there is a beautiful incident that I wish to discuss and share.

The contingent of monkeys and bears that are sent down south in search of **Mother Sita** reach the shores of the Indian Ocean. There they meet with the king of vultures, who pinpoints the location of Mother Sita in Lanka. The enthusiasm and happiness of the team having found the location of Mother Sita are quickly extinguished as crossing the vast Ocean seems like an impossible task. All the prominent members doubt their ability to cross the Ocean and return.

The majority of the monkey and bear team, led by *Angada*, accept defeat and decide to fast until death.

At that moment, the oldest and wisest amongst them, the Bear King, Jambvan, reminds Shri Hanuman of His divinely mystical prowess. Shri Jambavan narrates episodes from Shri Hanuman's fantastical childhood, helps Him recognise his divinity, and ultimately motivates Him to cross the Ocean and complete the designated task of reaching Mother Sita and delivering Shri Ram's message. The rest, as they say, is history.

Wise Counsel

The above incident in the Ramayana is testimony to the power of the right company. When you surround yourself with the right people, you can even achieve seemingly impossible tasks with sublime ease.

Everyone needs a Jambavan in their life. Someone who can remind us of our latent spiritual potential. A friend, a counsellor who can motivate and inspire us to fulfil our potential. Not everyone can have the power of Shri Hanuman (it's not even needed), and not everyone has the task of crossing oceans. But, in each person's life, there are situations where they need a pick-me-up.

"If speaking kindly to plants can make them grow, imagine what speaking kindly to humans can do."

Uplifting words are like nectar to the mind and the spirit. They nourish one's inner self that motivates them to act with vigour.

Choose Wisely

What kind of company do you keep?

Does your company inspire you to become a better individual?

Or does it debilitate?

The Vedic scriptures say that a true friend would even endure harsh words from the friend to bring them on the path of dharma (moral purpose and conduct).

When I was growing up, a few friends and I used to love watching the auditions for *Roadies* (hey, everyone has a past!). The most joyful part for us was how the judge, *Raghu*, used to insult the contestants. Upon reflection, I find it sad that sarcasm and putting others down have been made to appear cool by popular culture. **Chandler Bing's sarcasm** (a character from the American sitcom, FRIENDS) is immensely popular.

Do you remember when we were kids, our elders advised us to be around the studious students?

The elders were right that the company influences you.

Be around drunkards, and you'll become one eventually.

Be around those with a defeatist mentality, and you'll start thinking it's okay to have a victim mindset.

Associate with successful people, and their magnetism will uplift and inspire you to grow.

It pains me that most often, it's a person's inner circle that ends up harming them more than someone unknown. The most difficult challenge that one faces in life comes more from near and dear ones than from outside.

Look around your circle and find the ones who work to inspire through their conduct, words, and personalities. Be around such people, for their company itself can be a potential catalyst for your growth.

It is also essential to reflect on *how we interact with our friends?*

Do we uplift, enable, and inspire?

All change begins with oneself.

What you give out comes back to you such is the law of life.

Be that light for others, and seek that light.

Seek growth.

Choose to be the *wise bear*. (Wise Panda is taken, wink wink)

Thank you so much for reading until the end of the piece.

Love, laughter, harmony, and joy.

Death Talk : Part 1

"One who has taken his birth is sure to die, and after death, one is sure to take birth again."

BHAGWAD GITA, 2.27

When **Yuddhistra** and the other Pandavas were on exile, they encountered a **Yaksha** (a celestial being). The Pandavas had been looking for water when they chanced upon a lake. One by one, Yudhisthira's younger brothers went to the lake to fetch water but were rendered unconscious upon drinking that lake's water. When Yuddhistira went to the lake, the Yaksha told him that his brothers had perished as they failed to answer the Celestial's question. He warned Yuddhisthira that the same fate awaited him if he chose not to answer the questions and drink the water. Yudhishthira, the calm and wise man, engaged with the celestial. A wisdom-filled conversation ensues between the two. One of the questions that the Celestial asks Yuddhisthira is,

"What is the most surprising thing in the world?"

"The fact that people continuously die around humans, yet no one bothers to think of their mortal nature."

I'm sure you must have heard of the demise of two well-known actors in the Hindi Film Industry, **Shri Irrfan Khan and Rishi Kapoor, in** the past week (written in May 2020) Their deaths sent a wave of shock among those who had been touched by their work.

The Virus, which some estimates claim cumulatively weighs around a gram, killed a quarter-million people all over the planet in the last few months itself (written in 2020). The United States of America itself has lost more people to the Virus than it did in the **Vietnam War**.

What's incredible, though, is that most of us move on with sublime ease. People die, we mourn, and we go back to the status quo. Curiously, a phenomenon that's been consistent with human existence since its beginning fails to revoke us from our apathy towards the questions of human life.

Death is the ultimate reality of life. No one escapes death—no matter what race, caste, nationality, religion, or level of fame.

In some cultures, it is inauspicious even to utter the

word death. It's just as Yuddhisthira implied; we think other people die.

Curiously, in the **Bhagwad Gita**, death is termed a form of divinity.

"I am all-devouring death."

SRI KRISHNA, BHAGWAD GITA, 10.34

Why The Hullabaloo?

Death is not merely the end of life.

Death is an absence.

A perceptible being who had a unique, discerning mind and presence disappears at death.

Maybe death hits so hard because people live their lives as if they are eternal. Death is something that may happen someday, and usually it's a phenomenon that happens to other people. With each death, we move on and continue to live in denial of one of the fundamental aspects of life.

The **Srimad Bhagwatam**, the crown jewel of Vedic scriptures, states: The birth of an offspring should enable the parents to recall their mortality, just as the death of a parent (or elder) should awaken the child to mortality.

Movies like Anand and Kal Ho Na Ho present stories of characters who use the knowledge of imminent death to live profound lives.

Books like The Last Lecture and Tuesdays with Morrie chronicle the journeys of people who lived an even more meaningful life after being diagnosed with a terminal illness.

Although, aren't we all diagnosed with the condition of death the day we are born?

So, wouldn't it be a better choice to remember death (our mortality) each day of our existence?

A thought worth exploring and investing in.

Self-Enquiry

"Oh, she passed away." Often that's how we refer to someone who sheds their mortal body.

What passes away, though?

What is human existence all about, then?

Are we just a bag of chemicals?

Ramana Maharishi, one of the great sages from the land of Bharat in the modern era, used to base his teaching on one question:

"Who am I?"

Self-exploration and inquiry have also been the basis of all Vedic scriptures. One is encouraged to be a seeker of truth.

"I do not know" is the most profound statement on the path of self-exploration. Because only once you admit that you do not know do you create a space for longing to know.

How to seek, though?

How do we use death as a tool to further our spiritual evolution?

How do we even reconcile the existence of spirits?

Let us explore each of these topics further in the next chapter.

Wish you vibrant health and lots of laughter.

Death Talk : Part 2

I consumed two similar contents in the form of books: *A Man Called Ove* by Frederik Backman and *After Life*.

Both deal with a man trying to reconcile (and failing miserably) with the death of a spouse. Both the book and TV show are terrific. I cannot recommend them highly enough.

In the book, *Mr Ove* has had an incredibly fulfilling life with his *Sonja* (his wife). It was love at first sight for Ove. A tragedy (won't drop complete spoilers, as I would encourage you to read the book) keeps them childless. Yet the love between them is so profound that it never matters. They have lived until their old age, but now Sonja dies. Ove's entire life was centred entirely around one person. When she leaves, he is devastated beyond imagination. He wants to end his life.

In the Netflix show **After Life**, Tony's life loses meaning the day *Lisa* succumbs to Cancer. Lisa, his beloved wife, gave meaning to Tony's existence. Now that she's gone, he is eager to end his life. Only his love for his dog stops him from taking his life.

What's common between Tony, from After Life and Ove from A Man Called Ove?

Both struggle to reconcile the death of someone who gave meaning to their lives.

Misery ensues.

My primary takeaway from both the brilliant stories was that as long as you continue to attach yourself to matter (the body), you will be devastated.

Why?

Because matter has a beginning and an end.

Identifications

As long as we keep perceiving ourselves and others as only flesh and bones, there'll be trouble. (In fact, body identification itself leads to people doing all kinds of atrocities on the planet).

If one keeps considering their loved ones as a combination of blood, bones, and flesh, the cycle of misery can only end (hopefully) when we get the RIP tag. Humans have devised various ways to bid farewell to the bodies of those who pass away. Some burn, some bury, and some even leave the dead body for vultures to feast on. In **Vedic tradition**, the offspring is supposed to put fire upon the body of the deceased parent, the parent who spends all their life trying to protect the offspring. If you think deeply, you realize the rituals themselves are devised in a way to bring detachment and awakening.

Is Death A Necessary Evil?

Someone asked me,

"Which is that one TV show you wish never ended?"

As I thought about it, I felt there is not one TV show, or for that matter, anything else in life, that I'd wish were eternal.

The ending gives meaning to existence; ends help us appreciate more that which existed.

Sample the case when someone dies.

Mostly (and rightly so), people will speak in good terms about the dead. It's a pity that the dead don't get the opportunity to hear all the right things. When the body was alive, how much would she have craved to hear all the good stuff!

Death helps you reminisce about the good that life brought with its presence.

Is Detachment The Way?

Your near and dear ones are natural objects of love and affection.

Detachment doesn't equate with severing ties with people and wandering off into the mountains or jungles.

True detachment, as explained by **Shri Krishna in the Bhagwad Gita**, is *perceiving life beyond matter*.

One of the most revolutionary ideas presented in the Bhagwad Gita is that you are not the body—a spark, energy, dwells within the covering of matter that's divine. It neither gets created nor destroyed.

Enhancing Perception

"As a person puts on new garments, giving up old ones, the soul similarly accepts new material bodies, giving up the old and useless ones."

BHAGWAD GITA, 2.22

Approaching self-enquiry and analysis per Vedic thought will go something like the following:

If someone were to ask me, "Who are you?"

My first response would be my name.

But that's my name. That's not who I am.

I may proceed to tell the person about my sexual orientation.

"I'm a man (who's scared of lizards)."

Once again, that's my body

identification.

So who am I, then?

Some sample responses can be:

I'm human (species).

I'm an Indian (nationality).

Batman Fan (identification).

The mind (I have a mind, not am the mind).

The intellect (I have an intellect, not am the intellect).

And so forth.

A reasoned and patient analysis can lead any seeker to understand that there's a consciousness that dwells within. One may term it as *Atma, spirit, soul,* or *energy*. For simplicity, let's call it the observer or the witness.

This observer is always active, even in a state of deep sleep or while dreaming. When we wake up each day, this observer helps us identify with the body once again.

The matter is the (impermanent) residence of this observer.

Have we established this much?

Okay, let's see how to use this knowledge.

Perception Is Everything

Once you start identifying yourself and others as more than matter, a natural sense of detachment (from the body) arises.

Death becomes an occasion to rejoice in existence–a profound existence incapable of being replicated. Death becomes an opportunity to marvel at life.

"As the embodied soul continuously passes in this body from boyhood to youth to old age, the soul similarly passes into another body at death. A sober person is not bewildered by such a change."

BHAGWAD GITA, 2.13

Equality remains a utopian concept (and, in the case of communist ideology, a totalitarian concept) until we have a body-based identification.

In soul consciousness, there's a unity that religion, atheism, or humanity cannot achieve.

As a spirit, all are equal.

What happens after death is a matter of personal choice (and the subject of another post). One may think of heaven, hell, or liberation from cycles of birth and death. Whatever floats your boat.

To factually know what happens after death, one will have to die.

In **Harry Potter and the Philosopher's Stone**,

Dumbledore says (I am paraphrasing),

"To an organised mind, death is a great next adventure."

Would it be morbid to remind yourself of your mortality every day?

Not at all if one can develop and enhance the soul vision as advised by **Shri Krishna**.

Let death wake you up towards:

- Living a more profound life
- Loving and communicating freely
- Focusing on what brings joy to your inner self
- Being of service to life around

I hope my humble attempt at writing on the topic of death can present some useful ideas for you. Thank you for reading until the end of the piece.

May you live a vibrant life.

Journal Prompt: Reflect upon your ideas on death and how you approach the factual reality of mortality.

Gates Of Heaven And Hell

"From anger, complete delusion arises, and from delusion, bewilderment of memory. When memory is bewildered, intelligence is lost, and when intelligence is lost, one falls again into the material pool."

Bhagwad Gita, 2.63

Since childhood, anger has been one mental health issue that has been bothersome for me. The state of anger, as pointed out so rightly by **Lord Shri Krishna in the Bhagavad Gita** (refer to the verse above), robs you of your intelligence. As the divine Lord rightly points out, when intelligence is lost, one falls into a lower vibrational state.

The religious scriptures describe heaven and hell as geographical locations. The soul attains these destinations depending on the karmic merit that it has acquired during its lifetime.

But is that really so?

Can one stand at the gates of heaven or hell while embodied?

Are heaven and hell psychological?

Yes, if we were to go by a *Zen* tale.

A tale of a Samurai

Once, a mighty Samurai warrior visited a Zen master called *Hakuin*. He asked Hakuin,

"Can you show me the gates of heaven? I want to avoid hell; I wish to attain heaven. Can you please show me the way?"

Hakuin asked the Samurai about his identity.

"I'm the chief of Samurais. Even the king pays respect to me."

A Samurai is a perfect warrior. They are revered highly in Japan. Pride in the samurai was a natural consequence of his position.

Master Hakuin said, "You look more like a beggar than a Samurai."

This was a massive insult to the Samurai. His pride hurt and his ego wounded, he took out his sword, about to strike the master dead. He completely forgot why he had come to meet the master in the first place.

Hakuin laughed and said, "This is the gate of hell about which you wanted to enquire. The ego, the pride, and the anger help you open the gates to hell."

The Samurai understood what the master implied. He put the sword back in the sheath.

"*Here opens the gate of heaven.*"

This incredibly powerful tale helps us realize that **heaven and hell aren't geographical locations outside but psychological conditions within.**

When we are alert and act from a state of consciousness, the gate of heaven opens.

What happens when you are angry?

You're in a state of bewilderment.

You've lost consciousness.

In the story, as soon as the Samurai's pride is hurt, he 'loses his intelligence', his power to discern. He forgets why he came to the master. Given a chance, almost every human being would choose a pleasant to be in, not one where you lose yourself.

A recent discussion about the **Bhagwad Gita** with a friend led to us talking about anger. I recalled how one moment of rage lost Zinedine Zidane and the France football team, in the 2006 FIFA World Cup. Little blips in consciousness can lead to life-altering outcomes.

Relationships break, guilt perpetuates, and one loses a lot of potent energy. I have lost a lot of good merit on numerous occasions because of the mental health challenge of anger.

Become an observer

"It is lust only, Arjuna, which is born of contact with the material mode of passion and later transformed into wrath, and which is the all-devouring sinful enemy of this world."

Bhagwad Gita, 3.37

Anger, as Shri Krishna explains, stems from lust or a strong desire. In day-to-day life, I see it as a 'control issue' amongst us. When we try and determine the outcome and have preconceived ideas and notions about life; When we try to control others' responses and reactions—that's where we lose our element. No one can ever behave according to what we perceive as right or wrong. When that sense of control slips away, we burst out.

Emotions are the juice of life. They make you human, make you alive. When there are emotions such as compassion, love, joy, and gratitude, it's criminal to be possessed by a feeling that opens the gate of hell.

The question arises, though, should we judge ourselves or others on the merit of one emotion?

I have judged myself and, consequently, others for one lapse. Guilt has consumed me for certain parts of my life.

Has anything good come out of that?

Not once.

You cannot allow yourself to judge someone or yourself based on the smokiest chambers of your heart.

Usually, when you're in a lower vibrational state, such as anger, lust or greed, you end up doing the inconceivable. Those moments do not define any of us. Instead, what we can focus on is cultivating more moments of awareness.

Years of spiritual practice have led me to a conclusion: the training aims to make you detach from the drama of the mind and be an *observer*. Cultivation of awareness or the mode of observation needs practice, but Lord Krishna assures us that it is att, ainable and possible. A state of peace, calm, and contentment while residing in the body. A state wherein you influence your state of mind and environment more than the environment influences you.

I hope this piece was worthy of your time, dear reader. I wish you harmony, health, and well-being wherever you are. Stay in communion with your higher self.

Journal Prompt: When have you personally opened up the gates of hell for yourself?

My Toothbrush Anxiety

There's a place called Go Native in Jayanagar, Bengaluru. They have an awesome-sauce restaurant and a shop that sells a variety of products. The USP of the shop is that it deals primarily in Organic items and stuff that doesn't load the environment and planet any further than it already has.

Last year (2019), when I was there, I got myself a pack of two 'Bamboo Toothbrushes'. I have been using a Bamboo toothbrush for more than a year now. My small personal contribution to chucking plastic out of my daily life. I previously got myself one from Isha Life which I'd been using.

It's been 5 months (written in 2020) since I got them and have finally employed one of the two in use.

Now, not to bore you further with my shopping and choice of dental equipment, I will tell you what sparked the inspiration for this piece.

When I started using my '*amazingly attractive and certified organic*' new toothbrush, my mind filled with anxiety.

Why you may ask?

Because my extra-efficient, superb piece of evolutionary machinery called the mind started worrying about what will happen once I get through this toothbrush. It flooded me with questions like-

"How will you be able to procure the next toothbrush? No next visit to Bengaluru seems in sight..."

"Go-Native doesn't have an outlet in NCR..."

"What if you don't find an equally awesome toothbrush..."

Mind you all these thoughts when I have a spare toothbrush of the same kind.

Uncertain future

Once I noticed all these random thoughts floating in my mind-space, I couldn't help but laugh. Rather than enjoying the experience of using a new toothbrush, I'm allowing my mind to fill me up with anxiety over an uncertain future that may not even come into existence. I do wish myself a productive and long enough life to see myself plant a million trees (amongst myriad other things), but life IS uncertain. I may not even see the next daylight. There is a guaranteed expiration but no specific date for the human body.

This little episode with the toothbrush made me ponder how this anxiety over *what may happen* is a plague that most of humanity suffers from. Let's give it a term – **"Tooth-brush anxiety"** of '**TA**' in short. This TA is the number one cause that robs us of the joy of the PRESENT and creates scenarios that usually never come to pass in the head.

Think back on specific events in your life. For instance, Your high school/12th grade examinations, were called to be the defining moment of your life. I remember a few of my classmates coming out crying after the Physics paper in 12th standard.

I was smiling.

Almost everyone who was crying is doing better in their career than me (Even I am doing quite alright by God's grace at the time of this book going into publishing)

Back then, they would've been thinking–

"Mera toh zindagi barbaad ho gaya."

I can go on and list multiple such examples, but you get the point, don't you?

This **TA** is something that causes us to lose the essence of what is essential in the now. Of being grateful and appreciative of what already exists than fretting over may or what may not exists.

I want to illustrate my point by sharing a beautiful story from Yogic lore.

The Greatest Miracle

Once in ancient times, a man visited the Ashram of a renowned yogi in search of enlightenment. Bharat is the land of yogis, mystics, and gods. He had seen and heard several beings performing miraculous feats. While in the ashram, he sought a conversation with one of the leading disciples of the yogi.

He asked the disciple, "What is the greatest miracle you have seen your master do?"

"Can he walk on water?"

"Can he float in the air?"

"Can he magically make objects appear out of thin air?"

The disciple said that the master could do neither of the things mentioned above. However, the greatest miracle that he has seen his master do is—

"When he eats, he only eats. When he walks, he walks. When he is talking, he only talks. When he is meditating, he only meditates, and when he sleeps, he only sleeps."

Such a magnificent story about being present in every activity.

It truly is a miracle, especially for our day and age where there are tons of distractions and people's minds are easily agitated.

Personally, I have discovered that when I'm present and alert in the so-called 'non-spiritual' acts throughout my day, my meditations and chants, or spiritual' activities, become much more refined, easy, and joyous.

Practice *being in the now*, dear reader, and do not let this stupid **TA** get the better of you.

Be it a toothbrush, a commute, a meeting, a project, or anything else.

I wish you harmony, peace, laughter, and joy.

Journal Prompt: What is your toothbrush anxiety story? When have you put yourself in needless worry?

Power Of A Gaze

Our college had organised a cultural fest for the first time in our time back there in 2010.

My friend, Abhijeet, advised me to sign up for the **debate competition**. I complied, and when the curators asked me to choose a topic, for once in my life, I feigned confidence and said,

"Give me whichever topic you want; I know I'm gonna ace this."

I won the competition. First-ever time being 'first' in anything in life.

(That's why kids it's always good to *speak positive affirmations to yourself,* even if it's in jest. Also, a healthy reminder never to put yourself down, even if it's in jest.)

It's a sweet memory from my college life. In fact, one of the very best. Whenever I reflect upon it though, I cannot forget what actually ensured I ended up blabbering something about women's reservation with ease and confidence.

I was up against a senior from another department who seemed much more assured. As I got on the stage to speak, I had that funny feeling that you get below the rib cage often when your brain feels it's a desperate situation. We can term it anxiety, we can term it stage fright. You pick. I began speaking with haste and an intense pace. As if I was missing out on watching a live *Manchester United* game.

Although, what could have potentially been a disaster on stage was averted.

How?

I looked at my friend, Abhijeet, sitting in the first row of the assembled audience, and he just nodded his head kindly towards me and gestured for me to calm down and speak with ease. No words, **a mere gesture, and a reassuring look**. That's it.

Magic.

I did not pay heed to that funny feeling in my chest anymore. I do not even remember how the rest of the debate went.

I won.

I was also handed money (the envelope in which I received the the money is still preserved as a memento) as a reward for winning the competition.

My first ever earning: 1500 bucks.

I smile even as I write it.

Yet, what inspired me to speak with confidence?

One look: that's it.

Just one reassuring look from a friend and I got the confidence to win something for the first time in my life.

A Story From the Life of Tony Robbins

In one of his interviews, the top life coach on the planet, Tony Robbins, revealed that as a teenager, he and his family used to survive on precious little.

On one Thanksgiving day, the Robbins family did not even have food to eat. Miraculously, a kind stranger rang their bell to gift them some food. That episode had such a profound impact on Tony's life that he now feeds millions of people every year.

What started all of this?

One random act of kindness by a stranger. That one act of karma has now inspired a capable man to use his blessings to bring joy to millions.

Never Underestimate the Power of an Act of Kindness

When we think of our impact on the world, we feel it can only be done once we have millions of followers or from are in a position of fame; That's a debilitating idea. We do not need to be world-famous to add value to people's lives. We do not necessarily need to splurge millions to contribute to charity. Even one small act of kindness can trigger amazing transformations in people's lives.

Case in point: the two stories I shared above.

I'm certain that had my friend not given me that reassuring look when I started out with the debate, I'd have failed.

If someone didn't make Tony believe in the power of sharing, he wouldn't be doing the phenomenal work that he is doing right now.

(It also means that both Tony and I are amazing human beings who learn to receive good things in life with gratitude and grace. I'm also phenomenally humble, as is apparent.)

Never shy away from giving that compliment, extending that kind word, or doing your own small (potentially magnificent) bit to uplift the people around you.

Begin at home.

Begin with your friends.

I have always detested the idea that friends are supposed to only take each other's side and poke fun.

No, sorry, everyone else is capable enough for that task.

As a friend, uplift, motivate, and inspire.

As you form this habit, you can extend it to everyone around you.

The seed of karma is such that, more often than not, it doesn't sprout where it's planted.

You should know that it's a law of life that the vibrations of goodness sent out in the universe always find a route to come back when you are ready.

Do you have a story to share?

A random act of kindness from a friend, family member, or stranger that impacted you positively, or vice-versa?

I wish you joy, harmony, laughter, and peace.

Posing For Instagram

There is inexplicable joy in doing your thing, following your own path, and moving towards what comes easily and effortlessly to you. I was sitting and wondering about this thought today before I began writing this piece.

I use a phone application called 'Day One' to journal. I have linked my Instagram to the journal as well to remind me of the posts I made on the same day in preceding years.

Today morning, when I opened the application, I saw a post from 2015 that I'd made on Instagram. In that post, I'd shared a picture of the place called **India Habitat Centre**, where I used to perform plays for my theatre group. I could see I had used filters and a few other modifications on the picture to make it appealing and attractive.

I now laugh at the needless effort five (eight and counting) years hence.

Photography is not something that comes naturally to me. Neither am I interested in photography. But Instagram is, or at least was, a medium for people to share pictures of people, places, or things in a beautiful, appealing package.

I clicked a picture of the Habitat Centre in 2015, not because I wanted to but because I felt compelled to do so as others on my timeline were doing so.

Making efforts to win the approval of others hampers the spirit because, in the long run, such efforts mean zilch.

Being unaware of what comes naturally to us, allows us to suffer not just on social media but also in life.

In the past, I had a tendency to get jealous of the people who attracted attention and followers on social media. Thankfully, wisdom from **Shri Krishna** has me thinking on different lines. I find that most people who garner attention anywhere in the world, online or offline, do it by doing something that's authentic and what comes naturally to them.

You may say, "Kushagra, but don't you find people pretending a lot on social media?"

Yes, of course. But, perhaps even pretence comes naturally to some humans for they can sustain it for such a long period.

When I played this football based video game, FIFA, there used to be the option of creating a new player for your favourite team. While creating the player, the game asked us to select the kind of attributes the player has.

Is the player naturally gifted?

Is he a late bloomer?

Is he an early bloomer?

I have realized that in my life, I've been a late bloomer, or, as I'd say, I'm still wondering what it means to bloom.

As I 'bloom', I find the most joy in doing what comes naturally to me. In the case of social media, clicking pictures of food, clouds, and vistas is not natural for me. Even if, say, that garners more attention.

I no longer have to subject myself to the cruelty and harshness of seeking validation by doing things that I do not enjoy.

I do not have to make an art gallery out of my Instagram page.

(Respect and admiration to the people who manage to do it, though. They have beautiful creative talent and a lot of patience.)

I like sharing:

- My portrait pictures.
- Pictures of my friends.

- Pictures of Shri Krishna.
- Pictures of the books I read.
- I like sharing my written content.
- Any photograph that gave me joy while I clicked it.

How Do We Give in to the Ego and Dull the Spirit's Voice?

Saying yes to a career and relationship choice because society thought it was right for me.

Saying yes to an expensive car because this might win approval.

Saying yes to soul-dulling substances because that's somehow in vogue.

Heck, even saying yes to meditation if it doesn't come naturally just because so many around me tell its good.

Today's memory notification teaches me the vital lesson to 'follow' the instincts that feel natural.

Thank you for reading until the end of the piece.

Have you ever found yourself gravitating towards something that does not come naturally to you?

Stay vibrantly alive.

An Apologetic Wish

Birthdays are special. We are made to feel special by the people around us. Good, kind people. God bless them. It is an excellent occasion to express your appreciation for the person who's there in our lives. Some people who have the emotional bandwidth of a teapot and are as expressive (on screen) as Katrina are forgiven.

But, hey, largely, it is nice to share your heart's emotions with people on their birthday. A nice excuse to make people feel special and all that.

Because do we ever really grow up?

Does that little kid who vies for attention ever get over it?

Unless and until it attains some form of enlightenment,

I don't think so.

I had my birthday recently, and somehow birthdays have been a confusing event for me. I mean, it is a big deal that you appeared as a human on the day, and it is a good occasion to reflect at life and, well, inevitable death.

Birthdays in childhood meant getting your school friends home and playing cricket and video games with them.

Early adulthood led me to be around Shri Krishna and a few friends who were happy to accompany me to Vraj. Adulthood has meant experimenting more with solitude

There have been times I have been pissed beyond reason on certain friends who did not wish or call or do something I expected them to do. I mean, hey, it's a business deal, right?

HUMNE ITNA KUCH KIYA UNKE LIYE AUR UNSE EK BIRTHDAY WISH TAK NAHI HUA? 12 BAJE RAAT MEIN HUMAARI NEEND NAHI KHARAAB KEE UNHONE?

Basically, unki zindagi mein aur koi kaam nahi hai. Bas calendar pe nawab sahab ka birthday pe gola maarke, din kaate woh.

Expectations can be quite a bitch, you know.

I heard someone was put off by one of their best friends because they did not put up an Instagram story for them on their birthday. Such things have become important in our digital age, it seems.

Fair enough.

What irks and fascinates me at the same time, though, is the collective guilt of wishing someone a late birthday or forgetting their birthday.

When some people sent across their wishes through texts, I noticed how they were 'so sorry' for wishing me late.

It is good they were because it gave me material to churn out this piece (ha ha), but I am quite curious to observe how we as a society have nurtured this guilt in people.

Hey, someone is taking out their precious time to type out a wish, and they have to include an apology because somehow, in the past, people (including me) have induced guilt in others for not wishing them properly and 'on time'.

And 'on time' itself can have so many definitions.

For some, it can be midnight; for some, it can be first thing in the morning; for some, it can be thank you, dear Prime Minister Ji; because of you, I was born...No, not that. Sorry, I started typing like I was a current government minister.

I wonder now, what is more important?

Someone genuinely being there in my life for most of the year,

OR

A person making me feel special for one day of the year?

Life in the metros goes by at such a fast pace that you can post (and re-post) about an occasion in your life, and tons of people will view it. But as we labour on zombie-like in our lives, we fail even to send an emoticon reaction. We're so caught up in the frenzy of our own problems that it's genuinely is hard to be able to care.

Ever since this realization dawned upon me, I feel more compassionate towards myself and others when they don't wish to. And, it accentuates my gratitude for the ones who, despite their busy schedules, find time to share a text, a wish, a call (which I have to pick up because it will be rude to ignore calls on birthdays), or a mention on some social media platform—this may not be much, and it is just a normal thing for them maybe, but I feel so blessed to find people taking out even a minute to type a wish.

I'm grateful to Krishna for inspiring the idea that I, for one, do not wish to be a part of a group that piles on guilt on others for not doing 'enough' for me.

It is okay if you wish late. Thank you that you did.

It is okay even if you did not. Let there not be obligations.

Let there be no formalities.

And most importantly, let there be no clarifications about your being occupied with life.

Most importantly, if you expect something from

someone, better spell it out to them. Because contrary to common human perception, no one is a mind reader—especially the people who're close to you.

To all those who read this, whenever your birthday might be, whether or not I wish you 'on time' or post a 'story' or make a 'post', I wish you the best and when I do extend a wish, know that I actually sit in meditation to send you light.

Journal Prompt: Has it ever happened to you that someone not wishing you a happy birthday bothered you? How did you deal with it?

Suggestions From The Smiling Panda

Yes, I hear you.

You might be saying, 'Dude, literally the entire content of the book felt like suggestions from you.'

I have included a few suggestions in some of the articles that you have read, but I am still going to share some of the sources that have inspired me for the better over the years.

BOOK SUGGESTIONS:

Fiction reads:

1. Midnight Library by Matt Haig. (Or literally any book by him.)
2. Literally any book by Frederik Backman. Though Beartown trilogy is a great start.
3. Books by Sudha Murty are always a delightful and easy read. They are especially good for anyone who is looking to begin their reading journey. The books are easy to read and absorb.
4. One Hundred Years Of Lenni And Margot by Marianne Cronin.
5. Books by Taylor Jenkin Reid are what I term as 'masala entertainers'—Crisp writing and fun to read. My favourite is Malibu Rising.

Non-Fiction Reads:

1. Books by Malcolm Gladwell can very well make you fall in love with reading. I have loved all of his books, particularly, Bomber Mafia.
2. One Plus One Equals Three is a masterclass in creative thinking—Delightful anecdotal stories.
3. Conversations on Love by Natasha Lunn—So real and so impactful.
4. Atlas of The Heart by Brené Brown—Heart warming and educative.

Autobiographies:

I do not (yet) read too many autobiographies but I LOVED Trevor Noah's Born A Crime and Matthew McConaughey's Greenlights.

Educated by Tara Westover was equally fascinating and disturbing.

Self-Help Reads:

1. Atomic Habits by James Clear—An obvious choice.
2. Psychology of Money by Morgan Housel—Learned so much about personal finances from this book. On the same topic, an Indian book I loved is Let's Talk Money by Monika Halan.
3. Breaking The Habit of Being Yourself by Joe Dispenza—Some scientific talk around 'Law of attraction'.
4. You Can Heal Your Life by Louise Hay was an absolute life changer.

5. Books by Dr Wayne Dyer, particularly, Power of Intention, is a really nice read.

Spiritual Reads:

1. Bhagavad Gita. I suggest, if you already like Krishna and his stories, Bhagavad Gita As It Is by Swami Prabhupada will work as it is written from a pure devotional perspective. Bhagavad Gita by Eknath Easwaran is a more balanced take. God Talks To Arjuna by Paramhamsa Yogananda is mystical, deeply philosophical, and often hard to understand but you can give it a try if you are into yoga.
2. Ramayana and Mahabharata retelling by Krishna Dharma are authentic, magnificently narrated, and enjoyable reads.
3. Books by Shubha Vilas are also pretty amazing. He takes stories from Vedic scriptures and narrates them beautifully, including practical lessons that we can draw. I have learned a lot from him.
4. Inner Engineering and Karma by Sadhguru are good reads as well.
5. Mind Your Mind by Venugopal Acharya is again a gentle and effective spiritual read. I like to think of him as one of my mentors and am really grateful for his teachings and guidance.

I can send you a bigger and more exhaustive list of book suggestions on each genre if you want. Drop me a mail on:

kenshosandsatoris@gmail.com

THE WRITE ORDER

You Write. We Publish.

To publish your own book, contact us.

We publish poetry collections, short story collections, novellas and novels.

contact@thewriteorder.com

Instagram- thewriteorder

www.facebook.com/thewriteorder

www.ingramcontent.com/pod-product-compliance
Lightning Source LLC
LaVergne TN
LVHW041911070526
838199LV00051BA/2585